W9-AOK-984

Easy Dinners
SOUPS & STEWS

BARNES & NOBLE

NEW YORK

Pictured on front cover:
Tex-Mex Tortilla Soup (*see recipe, page 207*)

Pictured on back cover:
Sweet-Potato Pear Vichyssoise (*see recipe, page 248*)
Root Veggie Soup with Curry Croutons (*see recipe, page 127*)
Black Bean Chili (*see recipe, page 171*)

Previously published as
Grand Avenue Books *Easy Soups and Stews*

Copyright 2003, 2005 by Meredith Corporation, Des Moines, Iowa. First Edition.

This edition published for Barnes & Noble, Inc., by Meredith Books

All rights reserved. No part of this book may be used or reproduced in any
manner whatsoever without the written permission of the Publisher.

Printed in China

ISBN: 0-7607-6955-9

Great Soups and Stews for Everyday and Entertaining

No doubt about it—soups and stews make for some of the most satisfying meals around!

WHO DOESN'T LOVE SOUP? From chill-chasing chowders to summery gazpacho, some of the world's most beloved dishes are served up in a bowl. And for today's time-pressed cooks, soups and stews answer the call for special yet hassle-free meals. Many soups can be on the table in minutes, and even most slow-cooking stews require very little prep time—once you put the pot on to cook, you can sit back, relax, and savor the fact that a satisfying supper is simmering to perfection.

When it comes to the best soups and stews, the right recipe is everything. So here they are. Some—such as Pearl-of-an-Oyster Stew, The Ultimate Split Pea Soup, and Best-Ever Minestrone, were chosen because they're the best versions around for these ever-pleasing classics. Other soups attain "all-time best" status because they're utterly unique, one-of-a-kind recipes. You'll love selections such as Mushroom Tortelloni in Curry Cream or Sherried Salmon Bisque when you crave something well off the beaten path.

Great recipes sometimes cook quickly, too. For busy weeknights, you'll find an entire chapter of soups that can be brought to the table in 30 minutes or less. And when you want to bring out your best for entertaining, check out the festive selections in the Company-Special Soups and Stews chapter. Many, such as Country French Beef Stew and Caribbean-Style Pork Stew, were inspired by exciting flavors from around the globe.

Whether you're looking for a quick solution to tonight's dinnertime dilemma or the perfect entrée for a fun evening with friends, you have scores of terrific recipes to choose from. Each one is sure to bring winning results to your table. Enjoy!

3

Table of Contents

Soups and Stews Basics

Here's a little know-how to help you create satisfying meals for family and friends.
You'll find that once you master the basics, soup and stew recipes are practically foolproof!

Broth Options

Many soup and stew recipes in this book call for chicken, beef, or vegetable broth. In such cases, you can make homemade broth using the broth and stock recipes on pages 6 and 7. When pressed for time, you can call on one of these convenience products:

- **Canned Broths:** Use these convenient broths straight from the can. Low sodium versions are also available. When using condensed broths, make sure to dilute them according to package directions.
- **Bouillon:** Instant bouillon granules or cubes are available in beef, chicken, or vegetable flavors. For each cup of broth, mix 1 cube or 1 teaspoon of granules with 1 cup of water.

Blending and Pureeing Soups

When blending heated mixtures, cool the hot mixture slightly before blending. Fill the blender container no more than half full. Cover with the lid and open the vent. Drape a clean towel over the blender container while operating. Begin blending warm mixtures on low speed, then increase to higher speed, as necessary.

When processing heated mixtures in a food processor, fill bowl only half full. Cover lid with a clean towel while operating.

Storing Leftovers

To store leftover soups and stews, divide the cooked food into small portions and place in shallow containers. As a general rule, divide soups and stews into portions that are 2 to 3 inches deep, and stir them while cooling to speed the release of heat. Place them directly into the refrigerator. (Note: Never let perishable foods stand at room temperature to cool before they're refrigerated or frozen.) If the final destination is the freezer, transfer the cold food from the refrigerator to the freezer. Arrange containers in a single layer in the freezer until frozen; this allows the cold air to circulate around the packages, freezing the food faster. Stack packages only after they have completely frozen.

To reheat the soup or stew, place it in an appropriate-size saucepan. Cover and bring to a rolling boil, stirring occasionally.

Substituting Dried Herbs For Fresh Herbs

Fresh herbs bring a wonderfully fresh flavor to soups and stews. However, in a pinch, dried herbs can be substituted for fresh ones. To do so, use one-third the amount of dried herb for the amount of fresh herb called for in the recipe. (For example, substitute 1 teaspoon dried herb for 1 tablespoon fresh herb).

Before adding a dried herb to a recipe, crush it between your fingers and thumb to help release the flavors. To crush rosemary, use a mortar and pestle. Add dried herbs to recipes at the beginning of cooking time to allow their flavors to develop.

Basic Broth and Stocks

It's up to you—when you're in a hurry, make soups and stews using canned broth or bouillon. When you have a little extra time, call on a made-from-scratch broth or stock to add extra homemade goodness. Each recipe makes a big batch; leftovers can be frozen for up to 6 months.

Prep: 30 minutes

Bake: 30 minutes

Cook: 3½ hours

Oven: 450°F

Makes: 8 to 10 cups broth

4   pounds meaty beef soup bones (beef shank crosscuts or short ribs)

½   cup water

3   carrots, cut up

2   medium onions, unpeeled and cut up

2   stalks celery with leaves, cut up

1   tablespoon dried basil or thyme, crushed

1½ teaspoons salt

10 whole black peppercorns

8   sprigs fresh parsley

4   bay leaves

2   cloves garlic, unpeeled and halved

10 cups water

Beef Broth

Depending on the meatiness of your soup bones, they'll yield 3 to 4 cups of meat. Add this cooked meat to soups, stews, or casseroles.

1 Place soup bones in a large shallow roasting pan. Bake in a 450°F oven about 30 minutes or until well browned, turning once. Place soup bones in a large kettle. Pour the ½ cup water into the roasting pan, scraping up browned bits; add water mixture to kettle. Stir in carrots, onions, celery, basil, salt, peppercorns, parsley, bay leaves, and garlic. Add the 10 cups water. Bring to boiling; reduce heat. Simmer, covered, for 3½ hours. Remove soup bones.

2 Strain broth.* Discard vegetables and seasonings. If desired, clarify broth.** If using the broth while hot, skim fat. Or chill broth; lift off fat. If desired, when bones are cool enough to handle, remove meat; reserve for another use. Discard bones. Place broth and reserved meat in separate containers. Cover and chill for up to 3 days or freeze for up to 6 months.

***Note:** To strain broth, line a large colander or sieve with 2 layers of 100-percent-cotton cheesecloth. Set colander in a large heatproof bowl; carefully pour broth mixture into the lined colander.

***Note:** To clarify hot, strained broth, return the broth to the kettle. Combine ¼ cup cold water and 1 beaten egg white. Stir mixture into broth. Bring to boiling. Remove from heat; let stand for 5 minute. Strain.

Nutrition Facts per 1 cup: 20 calories, 1 g total fat, 1 mg cholesterol, 409 mg sodium, 2 g carbohydrate, 2 g protein.

Chicken Broth

What to do with the chicken meat? Look in the index for some ideas!

1 If using wings, cut each wing at joints into 3 pieces. Place chicken pieces in a 6-quart kettle. Add celery, carrots, onion, salt, thyme, peppercorns, parsley, bay leaves, garlic, and water. Bring to boiling; reduce heat. Simmer, covered, for 2½ hours. Remove chicken pieces from the broth.

2 Strain broth (see note, page 6). Discard vegetables and seasonings. If desired, clarify broth (see note, page 6). If using the broth while hot, skim fat. Or chill broth; lift off and discard fat. If desired, when bones are cool enough to handle, remove meat; reserve meat for another use. Discard bones. Place broth and reserved meat in separate containers. Cover and chill for up to 3 days or freeze for up to 6 months.

Nutrition Facts per 1 cup: 30 calories, 2 g total fat, 5 mg cholesterol, 435 mg sodium, 1 g carbohydrate, 2 g protein.

Prep: 25 minutes
Cook: 2½ hours
Makes: about 6 cups broth

3 **pounds bony chicken pieces (wings, backs, and/or necks)**
3 **stalks celery with leaves, cut up**
2 **carrots, cut up**
1 **large onion, unpeeled and cut up**
1 **teaspoon salt**
1 **teaspoon dried thyme, sage, or basil, crushed**
½ **teaspoon black peppercorns or ¼ teaspoon ground black pepper**
4 **sprigs fresh parsley**
2 **bay leaves**
2 **garlic cloves, unpeeled and halved**
6 **cups cold water**

Vegetable Stock

No meat needed for a rich, homemade stock.

1 Scrub all vegetables; cut off root and stem ends. Do not peel vegetables, unless coated with wax. Cut onions into wedges. Cut carrots, potatoes, parsnips, and cabbage into 2-inch pieces.

2 In a 6-quart Dutch oven heat oil over medium heat. Add vegetables. Cook and stir about 10 minutes or until vegetables start to brown. Stir in water, salt, dill, and pepper. Bring to boiling; reduce heat. Simmer, covered, for 2 hours.

3 Strain stock (see note, page 6). Discard vegetable mixture. Place stock in a storage container. Cover and chill for up to 3 days or freeze up to 6 months.

Nutrition Facts per 1 cup: 17 calories, 2 g total fat, 0 mg cholesterol, 313 mg sodium, 0 g carbohydrate, 0 g protein.

Prep: 30 minutes
Cook: 2 hours
Makes about 7 cups stock

4 **medium yellow onions, unpeeled**
4 **medium carrots**
3 **medium potatoes**
2 **medium parsnips, turnips, or rutabagas**
1 **small head cabbage**
1 **tablespoon olive oil**
8 **cups water**
1 **teaspoon salt**
½ **teaspoon dried dill, basil, rosemary, or marjoram, crushed**
¼ **teaspoon ground black pepper**

Sherried Salmon Bisque, **recipe page 20**

Here are some all-time great soups to kick off a meal or to serve along with a sandwich or salad.

Splendid Starters & Sides

Alpine Cheese Soup

Here's a best-ever serve-along—it goes with just about any sandwich, from roast beef or smoked turkey to ham salad! It's also plenty satisfying served simply with a tossed salad.

Prep: 25 minutes
Cook: 25 minutes
Makes: 6 servings

4 slices bacon, cut up

1 medium onion, chopped (½ cup)

1 stalk celery, chopped (½ cup)

1 medium leek (white part only), halved lengthwise and sliced (⅓ cup)

2 14½-ounce cans reduced-sodium chicken broth

½ cup quick-cooking rolled oats

¼ teaspoon ground black pepper

¾ cup shredded process Gruyère or Swiss cheese (3 ounces)

¼ cup whipping cream, half-and-half, or light cream

2 tablespoons snipped fresh parsley

1 In a large saucepan, cook bacon until crisp. Drain bacon, reserving drippings in saucepan.

2 Cook chopped onion, celery, and leek in the reserved bacon drippings about 5 minutes or until tender. Stir in chicken broth, oats, and pepper. Bring mixture to boiling; reduce heat. Simmer, covered, for 20 minutes. Remove from heat. Stir in shredded cheese. Cool soup slightly before transferring half of the mixture to a blender container.

3 Cover and blend cheese mixture until smooth.* Return to saucepan. Repeat with remaining cheese mixture. Stir in cream. Heat through, but do not boil.

4 To serve, ladle into soup bowls; sprinkle each serving with crumbled bacon and snipped parsley.

***Note:** For information on blending and pureeing soups, see page 5.

Nutrition Facts per serving: 161 calories, 11 g total fat, 33 mg cholesterol, 442 mg sodium, 8 g carbohydrate, 9 g protein.

HOT FROM THE POT

Don't let a cold bowl of chili or soup get you down! Keep soups and stews warm longer by serving them in warmed bowls. Just before ladling, rinse bowls under hot tap water; dry. Or, if the bowls are ovenproof, let them sit briefly in the oven at a low temperature.

Baked Potato Soup

You'll be surprised at how easy it is to bring this all-time-favorite restaurant soup home.

Prep: 20 minutes
Bake: 40 minutes
Makes: 6 servings

2 large baking potatoes
   (8 ounces each)
3 tablespoons thinly sliced
   green onions
⅓ cup margarine or butter
⅓ cup all-purpose flour
2 teaspoons snipped fresh dill or
   ¼ teaspoon dried dill
¼ teaspoon salt
¼ teaspoon ground black pepper
4 cups milk
¾ cup shredded American cheese
   (3 ounces)
3 tablespoons thinly sliced green
   onions
4 slices bacon, crisp-cooked,
   drained and crumbled

1 Scrub potatoes thoroughly with a brush; pat dry. Prick potatoes with a fork. Bake in a 425°F oven for 40 to 60 minutes or until tender. Let cool. Cut potatoes in half lengthwise; gently scoop out each potato. Discard potato skins.

2 In a large saucepan cook 3 tablespoons green onions in margarine until tender; stir in flour, dill, salt, and pepper. Add milk all at once. Cook and stir until thickened and bubbly. Cook and stir for 1 minute more. Add potato pulp and ½ cup of the shredded cheese; stir until cheese melts.

3 To serve, ladle into soup bowls. Garnish each serving with the remaining shredded cheese, 3 tablespoons green onions, and bacon.

Nutrition Facts per serving: 324 calories, 20 g total fat, 29 mg cholesterol, 561 mg sodium, 25 g carbohydrate, 12 g protein.

Hot and Sour Soup

Watch out—once you make this Chinese restaurant favorite at home, you'll have a hard time settling for the standard takeout version!

Start to Finish: 35 minutes

Makes: 6 servings

8 ounces fresh or frozen peeled and deveined shrimp

3½ cups chicken broth

1 7-ounce jar whole straw mushrooms, drained and halved lengthwise (optional)

¼ cup rice vinegar or white vinegar

2 tablespoons soy sauce

1 teaspoon sugar

1 teaspoon grated fresh ginger

½ teaspoon ground black pepper

4 ounces tofu (fresh bean curd), cut into bite-size pieces

1 tablespoon cornstarch

1 tablespoon cold water

1 cup fresh pea pods, halved crosswise, or ½ of a 6-ounce package frozen pea pods, thawed and halved crosswise

1 beaten egg

2 tablespoons thinly sliced green onion

1 Thaw shrimp, if frozen. In a large saucepan or Dutch oven combine chicken broth, mushrooms (if desired), rice vinegar or white vinegar, soy sauce, sugar, ginger, and pepper. Bring to boiling. Reduce heat and simmer, covered, for 2 minutes.

2 Add shrimp and tofu. Simmer, covered, for 1 minute more. Stir together cornstarch and the cold water. Stir into chicken broth mixture along with pea pods. Cook and stir until slightly thickened and bubbly. Cook and stir for 2 minutes more. Pour the egg into the soup in a steady stream while stirring 2 or 3 times to create shreds. Remove from heat. Stir in green onion.

Nutrition Facts per serving: 117 calories, 4 g total fat, 94 mg cholesterol, 877 mg sodium, 7 g carbohydrate, 14 g protein.

Lemon and Scallop Soup

Many of the best cooks use only fresh, seasonal ingredients in their soups. This new favorite takes advantage of spring's tender asparagus. Serve as a light entrée or a substantial appetizer.

Start to Finish: 25 minutes

Makes: 4 servings

12 ounces fresh or frozen bay
  scallops

1 cup fresh enoki mushrooms or
  shiitake mushrooms

5 cups reduced-sodium chicken
  broth

½ cup dry white wine
  or reduced-sodium chicken
  broth

3 tablespoons snipped fresh
  cilantro

2 teaspoons finely shredded lemon
  peel

¼ teaspoon ground black pepper

1 pound asparagus spears,
  trimmed and cut into bite-size
  pieces

½ cup sliced green onions

1 tablespoon lemon juice

1 Thaw scallops, if frozen. Rinse scallops; pat dry. Remove and discard stems from shiitake mushrooms, if using.

2 In a large saucepan combine the chicken broth, wine, cilantro, lemon peel, and pepper. Bring to boiling.

3 Add scallops, asparagus, shiitake mushrooms (if using), and onions. Return just to boiling; reduce heat.

4 Simmer, uncovered, for 3 to 5 minutes or until asparagus is tender and scallops are opaque. Remove saucepan from heat. Stir in the enoki mushrooms (if using) and lemon juice. Serve immediately.

Nutrition Facts per serving: 153 calories, 2 g total fat, 28 mg cholesterol, 940 mg sodium, 10 g carbohydrate, 20 g protein.

Pearl-of-an-Oyster Stew

For some families, oyster stew is traditional Christmas Eve fare—but why reserve it for just once a year? Try smaller portions as an elegant starter for a dinner party anytime during oyster season.

Start to Finish: 35 minutes

Makes: 8 servings

⅔ **cup sliced leeks**

2 **tablespoons margarine or butter**

3 **tablespoons all-purpose flour**

1 **teaspoon anchovy paste**

2 **cups half-and-half or light cream**

2 **cups milk**

6 **cups shucked oysters (3 pints)**

Several dashes bottled hot pepper sauce (optional)

1 In a 4-quart saucepan cook leeks in margarine or butter until tender. Stir in flour and anchovy paste until combined. Add half-and-half or light cream and milk. Cook and stir until slightly thickened and bubbly. Cook and stir 1 minute more. Meanwhile, drain oysters, reserving 3 cups liquid. Strain liquid.

2 In a large saucepan combine reserved oyster liquid and oysters. Bring just to simmering over medium heat; reduce heat. Cover and cook about 1 to 2 minutes or until oysters curl around the edges. Skim surface of cooking liquid. Stir oyster mixture into cream mixture. If desired, add hot pepper sauce.

Nutrition Facts per serving: 242 calories, 14 g total fat, 97 mg cholesterol, 248 mg sodium, 15 g carbohydrate, 14 g protein.

Sherried Salmon Bisque

Serve this unbelievable bisque with a crisp Caesar salad for an elegant and easy dinner. Or serve smaller portions as a lovely starter to a dinner party that features a rich, succulent roast, such as beef tenderloin.

Start to Finish: 25 minutes

Makes: 4 servings

12 ounces fresh or frozen salmon steaks, cut ¾ inch thick

3 cups sliced fresh shiitake or other mushrooms

¾ cup thinly sliced leeks or ½ cup thinly sliced green onion

2 tablespoons margarine or butter

2 cups chicken broth or vegetable broth

1½ teaspoons snipped fresh dill or ½ teaspoon dried dill

Dash ground black pepper

2 cups half-and-half or light cream

2 tablespoons cornstarch

2 tablespoons dry sherry

Fresh dill (optional)

1 Thaw salmon, if frozen, and cut into ¾-inch pieces. Discard skin and bones. In a large saucepan cook mushrooms and leeks or green onion in margarine or butter until tender. Stir in chicken broth or vegetable broth, dill, and pepper. Bring to boiling.

2 Combine half-and-half or light cream and cornstarch; stir into mushroom mixture. Cook and stir over medium heat until thickened and bubbly. Add salmon; simmer, covered, about 4 minutes or until fish flakes easily when tested with a fork. Gently stir in the dry sherry. If desired, garnish with additional dill.

Nutrition Facts per serving: 358 calories, 23 g total fat, 60 mg cholesterol, 562 mg sodium, 16 g carbohydrate, 20 g protein.

Shrimp and Coconut Soup (Sopa de Camarones con Coco)

The enjoyment-to-effort ratio on this Caribbean-style soup is unbeatable! Just five ingredients and about 15 minutes stack up to a terrific starter to a festive meal.

Start to Finish: 15 minutes

Makes: 5 servings

½ **pound fresh or frozen peeled, deveined small shrimp**

2 **14½-ounce cans chicken broth**

4 **ounces dried angel-hair pasta or vermicelli, broken into 2-inch pieces**

1 **tablespoon curry powder**

1 **cup canned unsweetened coconut milk**

Sliced green onion or snipped fresh chives

1 Thaw shrimp, if frozen. Rinse shrimp and pat dry; set aside.

2 In a large saucepan, bring chicken broth to boiling. Add pasta and curry powder; return to boiling. Boil gently for 3 minutes. Add the shrimp; cook for 2 to 3 minutes or until shrimp are opaque and the pasta is tender. Stir in coconut milk; heat through.

3 To serve, ladle soup into bowls. Sprinkle with green onion.

Nutrition Facts per serving: 268 calories, 14 g total fat, 69 mg cholesterol, 762 mg sodium, 22 g carbohydrate, 15 g protein.

Solid Gold Squash Soup

Winter squash soup is a classic, but with pulp to mash, it's sometimes a hassle to make. This easy-on-the-cook version streamlines the task by calling on frozen cooked winter squash.

Prep: 5 minutes

Cook: 10 minutes

Makes: 4 servings

¼ cup finely chopped onion

1 to 2 teaspoons curry powder

½ teaspoon ground ginger

1½ teaspoons cooking oil

2 12-ounce packages frozen cooked winter squash, thawed

1 cup chicken broth

1 cup apple juice or apple cider

¼ teaspoon salt

½ cup plain nonfat yogurt or fat free dairy sour cream (optional)

Finely chopped pistachio nuts (optional)

1 In a medium saucepan cook and stir onion, curry powder, and ground ginger in hot oil over medium heat for 2 minutes. Add squash, chicken broth, apple juice, and salt. Heat through.

2 To serve, ladle into soup bowls. If desired, top each serving with a swirl of yogurt or sour cream and sprinkle with pistachio nuts.

Nutrition Facts per serving: 126 calories, 2 g total fat, 0 mg cholesterol, 293 mg sodium, 27 g carbohydrate, 3 g protein.

Four-Onion Soup

With leeks, onions, garlic, and chives, this flavorful soup combines four ingredients from the onion family. Pair it with a crisp salad for a lovely luncheon main dish for six.

Prep: 30 minutes

Cook: 30 minutes

Makes: 6 servings

¼ cup margarine or butter

3 cups thinly sliced leeks (white part only)

4½ cups halved and thinly sliced onions

2 tablespoons minced garlic (12 cloves)

1 tablespoon sugar

6 cups chicken broth

1 teaspoon dried thyme, crushed

¼ teaspoon ground black pepper

2 tablespoons all-purpose flour

2 slightly beaten egg yolks

¼ cup Marsala wine or sweet sherry (optional)

1 cup half-and-half or light cream

Baguette-style French bread slices, toasted

Fresh chives (optional)

Fresh thyme (optional)

1 In a large Dutch oven melt margarine or butter. Stir in leeks, onions, garlic, and sugar. Cook, covered, over medium-low heat about 10 minutes or until vegetables are tender, stirring occasionally. Remove ¾ cup onion mixture; set aside. Add 5½ cups of the chicken broth, the dried thyme, and pepper to remaining mixture in Dutch oven. Bring to boiling; reduce heat. Simmer, covered, over low heat for 20 minutes.

2 Remove from heat; cool slightly. Transfer one-third of the mixture to a blender container or food processor bowl. Cover and blend or process mixture until smooth.* Repeat with remaining mixture. Return all of the pureed mixture to the Dutch oven.

3 In a small bowl stir together the remaining ½ cup chicken broth and flour until smooth. Stir in egg yolks. Gradually add 1 cup of the hot soup to egg mixture; stir mixture into remaining soup. Cook and stir over medium-high heat until thickened and bubbly. Add Marsala or sherry (if desired) and reserved onion-leek mixture. Cook and stir for 1 minute more; reduce heat. Stir in half-and-half or light cream. Cook and stir until heated through; do not boil.

4 To serve, ladle into a large soup tureen or individual bowls. Top each serving with a toasted baguette slice. If desired, sprinkle with chives and thyme.

*__Note:__ For information on blending and pureeing soups, see page 5.

Nutrition Facts per serving: 253 calories, 16 g total fat, 87 mg cholesterol, 893 mg sodium, 20 g carbohydrate, 9 g protein.

Smoky Corn Chowder

Flavorful smoked cheese is the secret ingredient that gives this version an edge! For smooth soup, be sure to use process cheese—it blends in better because it's less sensitive to heat.

Start to Finish: 25 minutes

Makes: 4 servings

1 10-ounce package frozen whole kernel corn

½ cup chopped onion

½ cup water

1 teaspoon instant chicken bouillon granules

¼ teaspoon ground black pepper

2½ cups milk

3 tablespoons all-purpose flour

1 cup shredded smoked process cheddar cheese (4 ounces)

1 tablespoon diced pimiento, drained

Canned or frozen baby corn, sliced lengthwise (optional)

Fresh chives (optional)

Chopped red sweet pepper (optional)

1 In a saucepan combine corn, onion, the water, bouillon, and black pepper. Bring to boiling; reduce heat. Simmer, covered, about 4 minutes or until corn is tender. Do not drain.

2 Stir together milk and flour; stir into corn mixture. Cook and stir until thickened and bubbly. Cook and stir for 1 minute more. Add cheese and pimiento; heat and stir until cheese melts.

3 To serve, spoon into 4 soup bowls. If desired, garnish each serving with baby corn, chives, and red pepper.

Nutrition Facts per serving: 223 calories, 5 g total fat, 27 mg cholesterol, 855 mg sodium, 32 g carbohydrate, 15 g protein.

Fresh Mushroom Soup

There are about as many cream of mushroom soup recipes out there as there are cooks who love to make it—but this version, which calls on oyster and shiitake mushrooms for extra flavor—ranks among the best.

Prep: 10 minutes

Cook: 10 minutes

Makes: 6 servings

8 ounces shiitake or button mushrooms

6 ounces small oyster mushrooms

1/3 cup chopped shallots

2 tablespoons butter

2 tablespoons all-purpose flour

1/2 teaspoon salt

1/4 teaspoon coarsely ground black pepper

1 14 1/2-ounce can vegetable broth or chicken broth

2 cups half-and-half or light cream

1/8 teaspoon ground saffron or saffron threads

Saffron threads (optional)

1 Remove stems from shiitake mushrooms; remove any tough or woody stems from remaining mushrooms. Cut large shiitake mushrooms in half; set aside. Chop the remaining shiitake mushrooms. Cut oyster mushrooms into large pieces.

2 In a large saucepan cook mushrooms and shallots in hot butter, uncovered, over medium-high heat for 4 to 5 minutes or until tender, stirring occasionally. Stir in flour, salt, and pepper. Add broth. Cook and stir over medium heat until slightly thickened and bubbly. Cook and stir 1 minute more. Stir in half-and-half and saffron; heat through.

3 To serve, ladle soup into bowls. If desired, top with saffron threads.

Nutrition Facts per serving: 193 calories, 14 g total fat, 40 mg cholesterol, 565 mg sodium, 15 g carbohydrate, 5 g protein.

Thai Peanut Soup

If you've ever been to a Thai restaurant, then you know all about the wonderful blend of flavors in Thai cooking. If not, consider this flavor-packed soup the perfect introduction.

Start to Finish: 25 minutes

Makes: 8 servings

⅓ cup finely chopped onion

⅓ cup finely chopped celery

2 tablespoons finely chopped red
   sweet pepper

1 tablespoon margarine or butter

3 tablespoons all-purpose flour

1 tablespoon very finely chopped
   lemongrass (white portion only)
   or 1 teaspoon finely shredded
   lemon peel

¼ teaspoon ground red pepper

1 14½-ounce can chicken broth

1 13½- or 14-ounce can
   unsweetened coconut milk

½ cup creamy peanut butter

1 tablespoon soy sauce

Chopped peanuts (optional)

Snipped fresh cilantro (optional)

Red sweet pepper strips
   (optional)

1 In a medium saucepan cook onion, celery, and finely chopped red sweet pepper in hot margarine or butter about 4 minutes or until vegetables are tender, stirring occasionally. Stir in flour, lemongrass or lemon peel, and ground red pepper. Add chicken broth and coconut milk all at once. Cook and stir until mixture is slightly thickened and bubbly. Cook and stir for 1 minute more.

2 Add peanut butter and soy sauce; stir until soup is well blended and heated through.

3 To serve, ladle into soup bowls. If desired, top each serving with peanuts, cilantro, and red sweet pepper strips.

Nutrition Facts per serving: 268 calories, 24 g total fat, 4 mg cholesterol, 395 mg sodium, 8 g carbohydrate, 7 g protein.

FRESH HERBS FOR A FINISHING TOUCH

Just about any soup can benefit from a sprinkling of colorful, flavorful snipped fresh herbs as a finishing touch. Experiment pairing your favorite herbs with your recipes. Parsley is a good all-around choice that works well with many soups; for soups imbued with onion or garlic flavors, try some snipped fresh chives. With tomato-based soups, try a light touch of snipped fresh marjoram, oregano, or basil. For creamy soups, try tarragon or dill. And, as an old cook's adage exclaims, "When in doubt, use thyme!"

In winter, when fresh herbs are scarce, consider swirling a little purchased pesto into soups to add a dose of freshness and color.

Yam and Peanut Soup

This soup perfectly pairs two classic ingredients often found in Southern cooking—peanuts and yams. It tastes great served alongside a ham sandwich.

Prep: 20 minutes

Cook: 30 minutes

Makes: 6 servings

3 cups peeled, sliced yams or sweet potatoes (about 1 pound)

¼ cup chopped onion

¼ cup chopped celery

2 tablespoons unsalted butter

4 cups reduced-sodium chicken broth

⅓ cup creamy peanut butter

¼ teaspoon ground black pepper

Chopped peanuts (optional)

Snipped fresh chives (optional)

1 In a large saucepan, cook yams or sweet potatoes, onion, and celery in hot butter over medium heat for 5 minutes, stirring occasionally. Add broth. Bring to boiling; reduce heat. Simmer, covered, about 30 minutes or until vegetables are tender. Remove from heat; cool slightly. Transfer half of the mixture to a food processor bowl or blender container.* Cover; process or blend until smooth. Repeat with remaining mixture.

2 Transfer all of the mixture back to the saucepan. Add peanut butter and pepper. Cook and stir over medium-low heat until combined and heated through.

3 To serve, ladle into soup bowls. If desired, sprinkle each serving with chopped peanuts and chives, and season with additional pepper.

*Note: For information on blending and pureeing soups, see page 5.

Nutrition Facts per serving: 133 calories, 11 g total fat, 11 mg cholesterol, 483 mg sodium, 4 g carbohydrate, 6 g protein.

Pesto-Vegetable Soup

This super-fresh recipe—made extra perky with pesto—is hearty enough to serve three as a main dish. Or serve smaller portions alongside a sandwich for a flavorful luncheon.

Start to Finish: 25 minutes

Makes: 3 servings

2 cloves garlic, minced

1 tablespoon olive oil

2 14½-ounce cans vegetable broth

½ cup dried ditalini pasta or small shell macaroni

1 cup packaged frozen stir-fry vegetables

3 cups torn arugula or Swiss chard, or shredded Chinese cabbage

2 cups torn spinach

3 tablespoons pesto

1 In a large saucepan cook the garlic in hot oil for 30 seconds. Add vegetable broth. Bring to boiling; add the pasta. Return to boiling; reduce heat. Boil gently, uncovered, for 6 minutes, stirring occasionally.

2 Stir in the stir-fry vegetables; return to boiling. Stir in arugula and spinach; cook and stir for 2 minutes more.

3 To serve, ladle into soup bowls. Swirl pesto into each serving.

Nutrition Facts per serving: 261 calories, 17 g total fat, 2 mg cholesterol, 1,281 mg sodium, 29 g carbohydrate, 7 g protein.

Roasted Garlic and Tomatillo Soup

From Mexico—with flavor! Try this colorful soup, featuring the slightly applelike flavors of tomatillos, as a starter to your next dinner party. Or simply serve alongside tacos.

Prep: 25 minutes
Bake: 20 minutes
Cook: 10 minutes
Makes: 8 servings

1 head garlic

2 teaspoons olive oil or cooking oil

1 pound tomatillos

3 14½-ounce cans chicken broth

¼ teaspoon ground black pepper

2 large tomatoes, cored and chopped (2 cups)

1 avocado, halved, seeded, peeled, and chopped

½ cup snipped fresh cilantro

1 cup coarsely crushed tortilla chips

4 ounces Chihuahua, queso quesadilla, or Monterey Jack cheese

1 Preheat oven to 425°F. Peel away outer skin from head of garlic. Cut off the pointed top portion with a knife, leaving the bulb intact but exposing the individual cloves. Place garlic head in a custard cup; drizzle with oil. Cover with foil.

2 Remove husks, stems, and cores from tomatillos. Cut tomatillos in half. Place cut side down on a foil-lined 15×10×1-inch baking pan. Bake the tomatillos and garlic for 20 minutes. Remove from oven and cool slightly.

3 Using your fingers, press garlic to remove paste from individual cloves. In a blender container combine half of the tomatillos, the garlic paste, and 1 cup of the chicken broth. Cover and blend until nearly smooth.

4 Transfer blended mixture to a large saucepan; add remaining chicken broth and pepper. Chop remaining tomatillos and add to pan along with the chopped tomatoes. Heat through.

5 To serve, ladle soup into bowls. Top each with avocado, cilantro, tortilla chips, and cheese.

Nutrition Facts per serving: 169 calories, 12 g total fat, 15 mg cholesterol, 758 mg sodium, 11 g carbohydrate, 6 g protein.

Farmer's Vegetable Broth

Forget mushy little bits of veggies commonly found in some soups—this all-time great version boasts hearty chunks of tender, garden-fresh root vegetables.

Start to Finish: 45 minutes

Makes: 4 to 6 servings

2 medium leeks, trimmed and
   bias-cut into 1-to 2-inch slices

1 medium rutabaga, peeled and cut
   into 1-inch pieces

1 medium turnip, peeled and cut
   into 1-inch pieces

1 small parsnip, peeled and cut up
   (⅓ cup)

1 small carrot, peeled and cut up
   (⅓ cup)

3 cups beef broth

3 cups water

½ cup dry sherry or beef broth

1 4-inch sprig fresh rosemary or
   ½ teaspoon dried rosemary,
   crushed

Fresh rosemary sprigs (optional)

1 In a Dutch oven combine leeks, rutabaga, turnip, parsnip, carrot, broth, the water, sherry or broth, and the 4-inch sprig of rosemary or ½ teaspoon dried rosemary. Bring to boiling; reduce heat. Simmer, uncovered, 25 to 30 minutes or until turnip and rutabaga are tender. Remove rosemary sprig.

2 To serve, ladle into bowls. If desired, top with additional fresh rosemary sprigs.

Nutrition Facts per serving: 123 calories, 0 g total fat, 0 mg cholesterol, 678 mg sodium, 18 g carbohydrate, 3 g protein.

Beet Borscht

Taste the beets before you add the sugar—then add as little or as much as you need for a smooth, balanced flavor in this classic favorite.

Prep: 20 minutes

Cook: 30 minutes

Makes: 4 servings

1½ **pounds beets, tops removed**

2 **small onions, halved lengthwise (about 8 ounces)**

1 **teaspoon salt**

5 **cups water**

2 **tablespoons sugar**

2 **tablespoons lemon juice**

¾ **cup finely shredded green cabbage**

1 Cut off all but 1 inch of beet stems and roots; wash. Do not peel.

2 In a Dutch oven combine beets, onions, and salt. Add the water. Bring to boiling; reduce heat to medium-low. Simmer, covered, for 20 minutes. Cool slightly. Slip skins off beets; discard. Cut beets into large pieces; return to liquid.

3 Stir in sugar and lemon juice. Return to boiling; reduce heat. Simmer, uncovered, for 10 minutes. Cover and chill, if desired.

4 To serve, ladle soup into bowls, using one onion half per serving. Sprinkle cabbage over soup.

Nutrition Facts per serving: 107 calories, 0 g total fat, 0 mg cholesterol, 700 mg sodium, 25 g carbohydrate, 3 g protein.

Potato and Leek Soup

Traditional potato soup gets a boost with the addition of sweet potatoes and a dash of nutmeg.

Start to Finish: 35 minutes

Makes: 4 servings

1 pound russet or Idaho potatoes, peeled and cubed

1 14-ounce can chicken broth

1 medium leek, cut into thin slices

1 cup sliced celery

2 tablespoons butter or margarine

2 cups peeled, cubed sweet potato

¼ teaspoon ground black pepper

¼ teaspoon ground nutmeg

1½ cups milk

½ teaspoon salt

Salt

Ground black pepper

Fresh herb sprigs (optional)

1 In a medium saucepan combine the cubed russet or Idaho potatoes and 1 cup of the broth. Bring to boiling; reduce heat. Simmer, covered, about 10 minutes or until potatoes are tender. Do not drain. Remove from heat; cool slightly.

2 Transfer potato mixture to a blender container or food processor bowl.* Cover and blend or process until smooth; set aside.

3 In a large saucepan cook leek and celery in butter or margarine for 3 to 4 minutes or until tender. Add the remaining broth, the sweet potato, the ¼ teaspoon black pepper, and the nutmeg. Bring to boiling; reduce heat. Simmer, covered, for 10 minutes.

4 Stir in pureed potato mixture, milk, and the ½ teaspoon salt. Cook and stir about 5 minutes more or until thickened. Season to taste with additional salt and black pepper. If desired, garnish each serving with an herb sprig.

***Note:** For information on blending and pureeing soups, see page 5.

Nutrition Facts per serving: 261 calories, 9 g total fat, 24 mg cholesterol, 819 mg sodium, 38 g carbohydrate, 8 g protein.

Italian Country Bread Soup

Instead of serving slices of focaccia with the soup, this recipe calls for it to be toasted into croutons and sprinkled on top.

Start to Finish: 25 minutes

Makes: 6 servings

8 ounces Italian flat bread
(focaccia), cut into ¾-inch cubes
(4 cups)

2½ cups chopped zucchini and/or
yellow summer squash

¾ cup chopped green sweet pepper

½ cup chopped onion

1 tablespoon olive oil

2 14-ounce cans chicken broth

1 14½-ounce can diced tomatoes
with basil, oregano, and garlic

Finely shredded Parmesan
cheese (optional)

1 Spread bread cubes in a single layer on an ungreased baking sheet. Bake in a 375°F oven for 10 to 15 minutes or until lightly toasted.

2 Meanwhile, in a large saucepan cook zucchini or yellow squash, green pepper, and onion in hot oil for 5 minutes. Stir in broth and undrained tomatoes. Bring to boiling; reduce heat. Simmer, uncovered, about 5 minutes or just until vegetables are tender.

3 Ladle soup into bowls. Top each serving with toasted bread cubes. If desired, sprinkle with Parmesan cheese.

Nutrition Facts per serving: 162 calories, 5 g total fat, 3 mg cholesterol, 869 mg sodium, 26 g carbohydrate, 6 g protein.

Soup with Mixed Pasta, **recipe page 82**

Ready in 30 minutes or less, these quick-simmering choices prove there's always time to gather around a comforting soup supper.

Super-Quick Main-Dish Soups

Italian Wedding Soup

There are many versions of this robust soup, but most combine leafy greens, meat, and pasta. This recipe calls on orzo, an almond-shape pasta sometimes known as rosamarina.

Prep: 5 minutes

Cook: 25 minutes

Makes: 4 servings.

12 ounces lean ground beef or lean ground lamb

1 small fennel bulb, chopped (about ⅔ cup)

1 medium onion, chopped (½ cup)

2 cloves garlic, minced

4 cups beef broth

2 cups water

1 teaspoon dried oregano, crushed

2 bay leaves

¼ teaspoon cracked black pepper

½ cup orzo pasta

4 cups shredded escarole, curly endive, and/or spinach

3 ounces Parmigiano-Reggiano or domestic Parmesan cheese with rind, cut into 4 wedges (optional)

1 In a large saucepan cook beef, fennel, onion, and garlic, uncovered, over medium-high heat for 5 minutes or until meat is brown and vegetables are nearly tender, stirring occasionally. Drain any fat.

2 Add broth, the water, oregano, bay leaves, and pepper. Bring to boiling; reduce heat. Simmer, covered, for 10 minutes. Remove bay leaves.* Reserve for garnish, if desired.

3 Stir in orzo. Return to boiling; reduce heat to medium. Boil gently, uncovered, 10 minutes or until pasta is just tender, stirring occasionally. Remove from heat; stir in escarole.

4 To serve, place cheese wedge, if desired, in 4 soup bowls. Ladle hot soup into bowls. If desired, top with reserved bay leaves (for garnish only—do not eat).

*Note: Bay leaves contribute a wonderful flavor and aroma to recipes; however, they should be removed before eating.

Nutrition Facts per serving: 262 calories, 10 g total fat, 54 mg cholesterol, 873 mg sodium, 22 g carbohydrate, 21 g protein.

Italian Beef Soup

Stock up on these ingredients over the weekend, then stash them in your fridge, freezer, and pantry. During the week, it will be easier than ever to drive past the drive-through knowing that this easy soup can be on the table in about 20 minutes.

Start to Finish: 20 minutes

Makes: 6 servings

1 **pound lean ground beef**

2 **14½-ounce cans beef broth**

3 **cups frozen pasta with broccoli, corn, and carrots in garlic seasoned sauce**

1 **14½-ounce can diced tomatoes**

1 **5½-ounce can tomato juice or ⅔ cup no-salt-added tomato juice**

2 **teaspoons dried Italian seasoning, crushed**

¼ **cup grated Parmesan cheese**

1 In a large saucepan cook ground beef until brown. Drain off fat. Stir in beef broth, pasta with vegetables, undrained tomatoes, tomato juice, and Italian seasoning.

2 Bring to boiling; reduce heat. Simmer, uncovered, about 10 minutes or until vegetables and pasta are tender.

3 To serve, ladle soup into soup bowls. Sprinkle each serving with Parmesan cheese.

Nutrition Facts per serving: 258 calories, 14 g total fat, 54 mg cholesterol, 929 mg sodium, 13 g carbohydrate, 20 g protein.

Heartland Steak and Vegetable Soup

Many of the best beefy soups are simmer-all-day affairs. Not this classic—it can be on your table in 30 minutes. (Maybe that's why it deserves all-time best status!)

Start to Finish: 30 minutes

Makes: 4 servings

2 4-ounce beef cubed steaks

¼ teaspoon garlic salt

⅛ teaspoon ground black pepper

1 tablespoon cooking oil

⅓ cup margarine or butter

1 medium onion, chopped (½ cup)

½ cup chopped carrot

½ cup chopped celery

½ cup frozen loose-pack baby lima beans

½ cup all-purpose flour

4 cups water

1 7½-ounce can tomatoes, cut up

½ cup frozen loose-pack whole kernel corn

½ cup frozen loose-pack peas

1 tablespoon snipped fresh basil or 1 teaspoon dried basil, crushed

2 teaspoons instant beef bouillon granules

2 teaspoons Worcestershire sauce

1 Sprinkle steaks with garlic salt and pepper. In a 4-quart Dutch oven cook steaks in hot oil about 3 minutes or until done, turning once. Remove steaks from pan and cut into cubes; set meat aside. Drain fat from pan.

2 In same pan melt margarine or butter. Add onion, carrot, celery, and lima beans. Cook and stir until onion is tender. Stir in flour. Stir the water into flour mixture all at once. Cook and stir until thickened and bubbly.

3 Stir in undrained tomatoes, corn, peas, basil, bouillon granules, Worcestershire sauce, and cubed meat. Return to boiling; reduce heat. Simmer, covered, about 5 minutes or until heated through.

Nutrition Facts per serving: 410 calories, 22 g total fat, 36 mg cholesterol, 924 mg sodium, 33 g carbohydrate, 21 g protein.

Easy Sausage Chowder

This chowder saves you time and trouble through the use of refrigerated shredded hash browns and pre-cooked sausage. The result is a quick, savory meal that only tastes labor-intensive.

Start to Finish: 20 minutes

Makes: 5 servings

1 20-ounce package refrigerated shredded hash brown potatoes

1 14½-ounce can reduced-sodium chicken broth

1 10-ounce package (2 cups) frozen whole kernel corn

2 cups fat-free milk

1 12-ounce package reduced-fat cooked link sausage, halved lengthwise and sliced

⅓ cup sliced green onions

¼ teaspoon ground black pepper

Salt

Green or red bottled hot pepper sauce

1 In a 4-quart Dutch oven or saucepan combine the potatoes, chicken broth, and corn. Bring mixture just to boiling; reduce heat. Simmer, covered, about 10 minutes or just until potatoes are tender, stirring mixture occasionally.

2 Using a potato masher, slightly mash potatoes. Stir in milk, sausage, green onions, and black pepper; heat through. Season to taste with salt and hot pepper sauce.

Nutrition Facts per serving: 264 calories, 3 g total fat, 26 mg cholesterol, 1,243 mg sodium, 42 g carbohydrate, 19 g protein.

Quick Corn Chowder with Ham

Here's one of the most filling and colorful versions of corn chowder around—and it can be on your table in just 25 minutes!

Start to Finish: 25 minutes

Makes: 4 servings

2 cups chicken broth

¾ cup sliced celery

4 green onions, chopped

⅛ teaspoon ground black pepper

1 16-ounce can whole kernel corn, drained

1 8¾-ounce can cream-style corn

5 ounces cooked ham, chopped (1 cup)

1 5-ounce can (⅔ cup) evaporated milk

1 tablespoon diced pimiento (optional)

½ cup packaged instant mashed potato flakes

Pimiento strips (optional)

1 In a 2-quart saucepan combine the broth, celery, green onions, and pepper. Bring to boiling; reduce heat. Simmer, covered, for 5 minutes.

2 Stir in whole kernel corn, undrained cream-style corn, ham, milk, and, if desired, diced pimiento. Bring just to boiling; reduce heat. Stir in potato flakes; cook and stir until slightly thickened.

3 To serve, ladle into soup bowls. If desired, garnish each serving with pimiento strips.

Nutrition Facts per serving: 453 calories, 9 g total fat, 21 mg cholesterol, 1,069 mg sodium, 76 g carbohydrate, 21 g protein.

Chicken and Salsa Soup

Tortilla soup has grown in popularity over recent years. While there are many winning takes out there, few recipes are quite as easy and flavorful as this one!

Prep: 20 minutes

Cook: 13 minutes

Makes: 4 servings

1¾ cups water

1 14½-ounce can reduced-sodium chicken broth

8 ounces skinless, boneless chicken, cut into bite-size pieces

1 to 2 teaspoons chili powder

1 11-ounce can whole kernel corn with sweet peppers, drained

1 cup chunky garden-style salsa

3 cups broken baked tortilla chips

½ cup shredded Monterey Jack cheese with jalapeño peppers (2 ounces)

1 In a 3-quart saucepan combine the water, chicken broth, chicken, and chili powder. Bring to boiling; reduce heat. Simmer, covered, for 8 minutes. Add corn. Simmer, uncovered, about 5 minutes more. Stir in salsa; heat through.

2 To serve, ladle into soup bowls. Top with tortilla chips and sprinkle with the cheese.

Nutrition Facts per serving: 319 calories, 9 g total fat, 42 mg cholesterol, 989 mg sodium, 32 g carbohydrate, 20 g protein.

Asian Chicken Noodle Soup

Comforting chicken noodle soup goes ethnic with the addition of Asian ingredients, such as soy sauce, fresh ginger, and pea pods.

Start to Finish: 20 minutes

Makes: 3 servings

2 14-ounce cans chicken broth

1 cup water

¾ cup dried fine egg noodles

1 tablespoon soy sauce

1 teaspoon grated fresh ginger

⅛ teaspoon crushed red pepper

1 medium red sweet pepper, cut into ¾-inch pieces

1 medium carrot, chopped

⅓ cup thinly sliced green onions

1 cup chopped cooked chicken or turkey (5 ounces)

1 cup fresh pea pods, halved crosswise, or ½ of a 6-ounce package frozen pea pods, thawed and halved crosswise

1 In a large saucepan combine broth, the water, noodles, soy sauce, ginger, and crushed red pepper. Bring to boiling. Stir in the red sweet pepper, carrot, and green onions. Return to boiling; reduce heat. Simmer, covered, for 4 to 6 minutes or until vegetables are crisp-tender and noodles are tender.

2 Stir in chicken or turkey and pea pods. Simmer, uncovered, for 1 to 2 minutes more or until pea pods are crisp-tender.

Nutrition Facts per serving: 224 calories, 6 g total fat, 58 mg cholesterol, 1280 mg sodium, 17 g carbohydrate, 24 g protein.

Easy Cheesy Vegetable-Chicken Chowder

With "easy" and "cheesy" in the title, is it any wonder that this creamy, colorful soup ranks among the all-time best soup recipes?

Start to Finish: 30 minutes

Makes: 4 servings

1 cup small broccoli florets

1 cup frozen loose-pack whole kernel corn

½ cup water

¼ cup chopped onion

1½ teaspoons snipped fresh thyme or ½ teaspoon dried thyme, crushed

2 cups milk

1½ cups chopped cooked chicken or turkey

1 10¾-ounce can condensed cream of potato soup

¾ cup shredded cheddar cheese (3 ounces)

Dash ground black pepper

¼ cup shredded cheddar cheese (1 ounce)

1 In a large saucepan combine broccoli, corn, the water, onion, and thyme. Bring to boiling; reduce heat. Simmer, covered, for 8 to 10 minutes or until vegetables are tender. Do not drain.

2 Stir milk, chicken or turkey, potato soup, the ¾ cup cheddar cheese, and pepper into vegetable mixture. Cook and stir over medium heat until cheese melts and mixture is heated through.

3 To serve, ladle soup into bowls; sprinkle each serving with the remaining cheddar cheese.

Nutrition Facts per serving: 380 calories, 18 g total fat, 94 mg cholesterol, 970 mg sodium, 25 g carbohydrate, 31 g protein.

Cream of Chile-Chicken Soup

To shave prep time, this tasty recipe starts with a can of soup and gets remarkably more interesting thanks to all the easy and delicious stir-ins you add to it.

Start to Finish: 30 minutes

Makes: 4 servings

8 ounces uncooked ground chicken
   or turkey

¼ cup chopped onion

2 cloves garlic, minced

2 cups milk

1 10¾-ounce can condensed cream
   of chicken soup

1 7-ounce can whole kernel corn
   with sweet peppers, drained

1 medium tomato, chopped (½ cup)

1 4-ounce can diced green chile
   peppers, drained

2 tablespoons snipped fresh
   cilantro or parsley

¼ teaspoon ground red pepper

1 cup shredded Monterey Jack
   cheese (4 ounces)

1 In a large saucepan or Dutch oven cook ground chicken or turkey, onion, and garlic until chicken or turkey is no longer pink and onion is tender. Drain fat, if necessary.

2 Stir in milk, cream of chicken soup, corn, chopped tomato, chile peppers, cilantro or parsley, and ground red pepper. Bring to boiling; reduce heat. Simmer, uncovered, for 5 minutes, stirring occasionally.

3 Add Monterey Jack cheese. Cook and stir until cheese is melted.

Nutrition Facts per serving: 375 calories, 19 g total fat, 68 mg cholesterol, 1,481 mg sodium, 29 g carbohydrate, 24 g protein.

Quick Turkey and Rice Soup

No recipe collection would be complete without a delicious idea for leftover holiday turkey. Here's a classic! If you don't have leftover turkey or chicken, see tip, page 70.

Start to Finish: 25 minutes

Makes: 6 servings

4 cups chicken broth

1 cup water

¼ teaspoon dried rosemary, crushed

¼ teaspoon ground black pepper

1 10-ounce package frozen mixed vegetables

1 cup quick-cooking white rice

2 cups chopped cooked turkey or chicken

1 14½-ounce can tomatoes, cut up

1 In a large saucepan combine chicken broth, the water, rosemary, and pepper. Bring to boiling. Stir in mixed vegetables and rice.

2 Return to boiling; reduce heat. Simmer, covered, for 10 to 15 minutes or until vegetables and rice are tender. Stir in turkey or chicken and undrained tomatoes. Heat through.

Nutrition Facts per serving: 209 calories, 4 g total fat, 36 mg cholesterol, 699 mg sodium, 24 g carbohydrate, 20 g protein.

Creamy Broccoli-Chicken Soup

Leftover chicken or turkey makes this satisfying soup irresistibly quick and flavorful. No leftovers on hand? See the tip below.

Start to Finish: 20 minutes

Makes: 4 servings

1½ cups small broccoli florets

 1 cup sliced fresh mushrooms

½ cup shredded carrot

¼ cup chopped onion

¼ cup margarine or butter

¼ cup all-purpose flour

1½ teaspoons snipped fresh basil or
    ½ teaspoon dried basil, crushed

¼ teaspoon ground black pepper

 3 cups milk

 1 cup half-and-half or light cream

 1 tablespoon white wine
    Worcestershire sauce

1½ teaspoons instant chicken
    bouillon granules

1½ cups chopped cooked chicken or
    turkey

1 In a medium saucepan cook and stir broccoli, mushrooms, carrot, and onion in hot margarine or butter for 6 to 8 minutes or until vegetables are tender.

2 Stir in flour, basil, and pepper. Add milk and half-and-half or light cream all at once; add white wine, Worcestershire sauce, and bouillon granules. Cook and stir until thickened and bubbly. Stir in chicken or turkey; heat through.

Nutrition Facts per serving: 435 calories, 26 g total fat, 86 mg cholesterol, 675 mg sodium, 23 g carbohydrate, 27 g protein.

COOKING CHICKEN FOR SOUPS

Soup is a tasty way to use up leftover poultry. But if you don't have any on hand, consider these options for cooked chicken:

- Purchase a roasted chicken from your supermarket's deli section. A roasted chicken will yield 1½ to 2 cups boneless chopped meat.
- Search the freezer case for frozen chopped pre-cooked chicken breasts; thaw in the refrigerator before using.
- Another option is to cook your own chicken breasts. In a large skillet place 12 ounces skinless, boneless chicken breasts and 1½ cups water. Bring to boiling; reduce heat. Simmer, covered, for 12 to 14 minutes or until chicken is no longer pink (170°F). Drain well. Cut up chicken as recipe directs. The yield will be about 2 cups cubed, cooked chicken.

Turkey and Sweet Potato Chowder

This soup makes the perfect day-after-the-holiday dinner. Of course, you can make it any time of year with purchased cooked turkey breast.

Start to Finish: 35 minutes

Makes: 4 servings

1 large potato, peeled and chopped (about 1½ cups)

1 14½-ounce can chicken broth

2 small frozen ears of corn on the cob, thawed

12 ounces cooked turkey breast, cut into ½-inch cubes (2¼ cups)

1½ cups milk

1 large sweet potato, peeled and cut into ¾-inch cubes (about 1½ cups)

¼ teaspoon ground black pepper

¼ cup coarsely snipped fresh Italian parsley

1 In a 3-quart saucepan combine chopped potato and chicken broth. Bring just to boiling; reduce heat. Simmer, uncovered, about 12 minutes or until potato is tender, stirring occasionally. Remove from heat. Using potato masher, mash potato until mixture is thickened and smooth.

2 Cut the kernels from one of the ears of corn. Carefully cut the second ear of corn crosswise into ½-inch circles.

3 Stir corn, turkey, milk, sweet potato, and pepper into potato mixture in saucepan. Bring to boiling; reduce heat. Cook, uncovered, for 12 to 15 minutes or until the sweet potato is tender.

4 To serve, ladle chowder into bowls. Sprinkle with parsley.

Nutrition Facts per serving: 309 calories, 5 g total fat, 66 mg cholesterol, 381 mg sodium, 32 g carbohydrate, 33 g protein.

Effortless Shrimp Chowder

Six ingredients (five, if you omit the optional cilantro garnish!) and a few minutes are all you need to transform a can of soup into this fresh-tasting, full-flavored chowder. Serve with hot garlic bread and a crisp salad.

Prep: 5 minutes

Cook: 6 minutes

Makes: 4 servings

1 10¾-ounce can condensed cream of shrimp soup

1 cup milk, half-and-half, or light cream

¼ cup cream sherry or dry sherry (not cooking sherry)

1 tablespoon margarine or butter (optional)

8 ounces fresh or frozen small shrimp, peeled and deveined (about 1 cup)

Fresh cilantro sprigs (optional)

1 In a 2-quart saucepan combine soup, milk, and sherry. Bring just to boiling. If desired, add margarine or butter. Reduce heat. Simmer, uncovered, for 5 minutes, stirring often. Chop shrimp, if desired. Add shrimp to mixture; return to boiling.

2 Reduce heat. Simmer for 1 to 2 minutes or until shrimp are opaque.

3 To serve, ladle into bowls. If desired, garnish with cilantro sprigs.

Nutrition Facts per serving: 138 calories, 5 g total fat, 80 mg cholesterol, 699 mg sodium, 9 g carbohydrate, 11 g protein.

North Sea Chowder

Fish chowders like this one are great busy-night fare because they cook up quickly. Keep the staples on hand and stop off at the fish market on your way home from work. Dinner can be on the table in just 20 minutes.

Start to Finish: 20 minutes

Makes: 4 to 6 servings

½ **cup chopped onion**

2 **cloves garlic, minced**

1 **tablespoon butter or olive oil**

4 **cups water**

2 **fish bouillon cubes**

1 **tablespoon lemon juice**

½ **teaspoon instant chicken bouillon granules**

½ **teaspoon dried thyme, crushed**

¼ **teaspoon fennel seeds**

Dash powdered saffron (optional)

1 **bay leaf**

1 **pound skinless, boneless sea bass, red snapper, and/or catfish fillets, cut into ¾-inch cubes**

4 **Roma tomatoes, halved lengthwise and thinly sliced**

Fresh thyme sprigs (optional)

1 In a large saucepan cook onion and garlic in hot butter or olive oil over medium heat until tender. Stir in the water, fish bouillon cubes, lemon juice, chicken bouillon granules, thyme, fennel, saffron (if desired), and bay leaf. Cook and stir until boiling.

2 Add fish and tomatoes. Return to boiling; reduce heat. Simmer, covered, for 10 minutes or until fish flakes easily when tested with a fork. Discard bay leaf.

3 To serve, ladle soup into bowls. If desired, garnish with fresh thyme.

Nutrition Facts per serving: 160 calories, 5 g total fat, 55 mg cholesterol, 683 mg sodium, 6 g carbohydrate, 22 g protein.

Chunky Vegetable-Cod Soup

A trio of herbs gives this hearty fish soup fresh-from-the-garden flavor with lots of family appeal.

Start to Finish: **25 minutes**

Makes: **4 servings**

1 **pound fresh or frozen skinless cod fillets or steaks**

½ **cup chopped red sweet pepper**

¼ **cup chopped onion**

1 **tablespoon margarine or butter**

3½ **cups vegetable broth or chicken broth**

1 **cup frozen cut green beans**

1 **cup coarsely chopped cabbage**

½ **cup sliced carrot**

1 **teaspoon snipped fresh basil**

1 **teaspoon snipped fresh thyme**

½ **teaspoon snipped fresh rosemary**

¼ **teaspoon ground black pepper**

1 Thaw fish, if frozen and cut into 1-inch pieces. In a large saucepan or Dutch oven cook red pepper and onion in margarine until tender.

2 Stir in broth, green beans, cabbage, carrot, basil, thyme, rosemary, and black pepper. Bring to boiling; reduce heat. Simmer, covered, for 8 to 10 minutes or until vegetables are nearly tender.

3 Stir fish into broth mixture. Return to boiling; reduce heat. Simmer, covered, about 5 minutes or until fish flakes easily when tested with a fork, stirring once.

Nutrition Facts per serving: 140 calories, 5 g total fat, 45 mg cholesterol, 922 mg sodium, 9 g carbohydrate, 20 g protein.

Spicy Shrimp and Noodle Soup

How do you get one pound of shrimp to serve six? Stir in ramen noodles, black beans, and just the right seasonings for a hearty and flavor-packed one-dish meal.

Start to Finish: 35 minutes

Makes: 6 servings

- 1 **pound fresh or frozen medium shrimp in shells**
- 1 **tablespoon lemon juice**
- ¼ **teaspoon chili powder**
- ¼ **teaspoon ground cumin**
- ⅛ **teaspoon ground black pepper**
- 5 **cups water**
- 2 **3-ounce packages shrimp- or oriental-flavored ramen noodles**
- 1 **16-ounce jar salsa (about 1¾ cups)**
- 1 **15-ounce can black beans, rinsed and drained**
- 1 **8¾-ounce can no-salt-added whole kernel corn, drained**
- ¼ **cup snipped fresh cilantro**
- 1 **green onion, thinly sliced**
  Shredded cheddar cheese (optional)
  Snipped fresh cilantro (optional)

1 Thaw shrimp, if frozen. Peel and devein shrimp, leaving tails on if desired. In a medium bowl combine lemon juice, chili powder, cumin, and pepper; add shrimp. Toss to coat. Refrigerate shrimp for 20 minutes, stirring occasionally.

2 Meanwhile, in a large saucepan bring the water to boiling. Stir in one of the noodle flavor packets (reserve remaining flavor packet for another use). Break ramen noodles into pieces; add to saucepan. Return to boiling; cook for 1 minute. Add the shrimp; cook for 1 to 2 minutes more or until shrimp are opaque. Stir in salsa, beans, corn, snipped cilantro, and green onion. Heat through.

3 To serve, ladle into soup bowls. If desired, top each serving with a little shredded cheese and garnish with snipped fresh cilantro.

Nutrition Facts per serving: 251 calories, 6 g total fat, 92 mg cholesterol, 976 mg sodium, 33 g carbohydrate, 20 g protein.

Soup with Mixed Pasta

Ever wonder what to do with all those bits and bobs of leftover pasta you have in your cupboard? Wonder no more—stir them into this quick soup.

Start to Finish: 30 minutes

Makes: 3 servings

4 cups reduced-sodium chicken broth

1 cup water

1 large onion, chopped (1 cup)

1 large carrot, chopped (¾ cup)

4 cloves garlic, minced

3 bay leaves

4 ounces skinless, boneless chicken breast halves, coarsely chopped.

1 teaspoon olive oil or cooking oil

2 ounces small dried pasta (such as rotini, ditalini, fusilli, wagon wheel or shell macaroni, and/or broken spaghetti)

Fresh sage leaves

1 In a large saucepan bring chicken broth and the water to boiling. Add onion, carrot, garlic, and bay leaves; reduce heat. Simmer, uncovered, for 10 minutes.

2 In a medium skillet cook and stir the chicken in hot oil over medium-high heat about 2 minutes or until no longer pink.

3 Add chicken, pasta, and sage to broth mixture. Simmer, uncovered, for 8 to 10 minutes or until the larger pieces of pasta are tender but still firm. Discard bay leaves.

Nutrition Facts per serving: 220 calories, 6 g total fat, 20 mg cholesterol, 896 mg sodium, 28 g carbohydrate, 14 g protein.

Take-It-Easy Posole

This main-course Mexican stew is often made with pork and sometimes simmered all day. Here's an equally hearty fuss-free meatless version that cooks in just 30 minutes.

Prep: 5 minutes

Cook: 30 minutes

Makes: 3 servings

1 6¾-ounce package Spanish rice pilaf mix

1 14½-ounce can vegetable broth or reduced-sodium chicken broth

1 cup water

1 teaspoon dried oregano, crushed

½ teaspoon ground cumin

1 14½-ounce can golden hominy, rinsed and drained

1 4-ounce can diced green chile peppers

1 16-ounce can low-sodium tomatoes, cut up

½ cup snipped fresh cilantro

Fat-free dairy sour cream (optional)

Snipped fresh cilantro (optional)

1 In a large saucepan combine rice mix, seasoning packet, broth, the water, oregano, and cumin. Bring to boiling; reduce heat. Simmer, covered, for 25 minutes. Add hominy and undrained chile peppers. Continue cooking about 5 minutes more or until rice is tender. Stir in undrained tomatoes and the ½ cup cilantro. Cook and stir until heated through.

2 To serve, ladle soup into soup bowls. If desired, garnish with sour cream and additional snipped cilantro.

Nutrition Facts per serving: 353 calories, 4 g total fat, 0 mg cholesterol, 2,075 mg sodium, 76 g carbohydrate, 10 g protein.

Jalapeño Corn Chowder

Here's a festive Southwestern take on the ever-popular corn chowder. Pair it with corn bread and coleslaw for a lively, yet easygoing supper.

Start to Finish: 20 minutes

Makes: 4 servings

3 cups frozen whole kernel corn or 3 cups fresh corn kernels (cut from 6 to 7 ears of corn)

1 14½-ounce can chicken broth

1¼ cups cooked small pasta (such as ditalini or tiny shell macaroni)

1 cup milk, half-and-half, or light cream

¼ of a 7-ounce jar roasted red sweet peppers, drained and chopped (¼ cup)

1 or 2 fresh jalapeño chile peppers, seeded and finely chopped (see tip, page 176)

½ cup crumbled feta cheese (optional)

1 In a blender container or food processor bowl combine half of the corn and chicken broth. Cover; blend or process until almost smooth.

2 In a large saucepan combine the broth mixture and the remaining corn. If using fresh corn, bring to boiling; reduce heat. Simmer, covered, for 2 to 3 minutes or until corn is crisp-tender.

3 Stir in cooked pasta, milk, roasted sweet peppers, and jalapeño peppers; heat through.

4 To serve, ladle into soup bowls. If desired, top with feta cheese.

Nutrition Facts per serving: 247 calories, 3 g total fat, 5 mg cholesterol, 363 mg sodium, 47 g carbohydrate, 11 g protein.

Succotash Soup and Dumplings, **recipe page 116**

Put the pot on to boil! Satisfying everyday suppers start with this array of rib-sticking recipes.

Home-Style Main-Dish Soups

Beef-Vegetable Soup

This satisfying chili-flavored dish brims with chunks of beef and a basketful of vegetables. Lengthy simmering of the beef shanks helps bring out its hallmark rich, meaty flavor.

Prep: 35 minutes

Cook: 2½ hours

Makes: 8 servings

3 pounds meaty beef shank crosscuts

2 tablespoons cooking oil

6 cups water

2 cups tomato juice

4 teaspoons instant beef bouillon granules

1 tablespoon Worcestershire sauce

1 teaspoon chili powder

2 bay leaves

2 medium carrots, diagonally sliced (1 cup)

2 stalks celery, sliced (1 cup)

1 medium potato, peeled and cubed (1 cup)

1 cup coarsely chopped cabbage

1 small onion, coarsely chopped (⅓ cup)

1 In a 4-quart Dutch oven brown meat, half at a time, in the hot oil; drain off fat. Return all meat to pan. Stir in the water, tomato juice, beef bouillon granules, Worcestershire sauce, chili powder, and bay leaves. Bring to boiling; reduce heat. Simmer, covered, for 2 hours. Remove beef crosscuts. Skim fat from broth.

2 When cool enough to handle, remove meat from bones; discard bones. Coarsely chop meat.

3 Stir chopped meat, carrots, celery, potato, cabbage, and onion into broth. Bring to boiling; reduce heat. Simmer, covered, for 30 to 45 minutes or until vegetables and beef are tender. Discard bay leaves.

Nutrition Facts per serving: 185 calories, 5 g total fat, 55 mg cholesterol, 743 mg sodium, 9 g carbohydrate, 26 g protein.

Hearty Mushroom and Beef Soup

Here's a classic that's always in style and sets the stage for a cozy family supper.

Prep: 20 minutes

Cook: 1 hour 10 minutes

Makes: 4 servings

1 tablespoon cooking oil

1 pound boneless beef chuck, cut
    into ½-inch cubes

1 medium onion, chopped (½ cup)

3 cups beef broth

½ of a 28-ounce can (1¾ cups)
    crushed tomatoes

8 ounces fresh mushrooms, sliced

¾ teaspoon dried oregano, crushed

¾ teaspoon bottled minced garlic

1 bay leaf

½ cup sliced carrot

2 tablespoons cold water

4 teaspoons cornstarch

1 cup cooked rice

¼ cup dry red wine (optional)

   Fresh herb sprigs, such as
      rosemary, oregano, or parsley
      (optional)

1 In large saucepan or Dutch oven, heat oil over medium-high heat; add half of the meat. Cook and stir 2 to 3 minutes or until brown. Remove with slotted spoon. Repeat with remaining meat and the onion. Return all meat to pan. Stir in beef broth, crushed tomatoes, mushrooms, oregano, garlic, and bay leaf. Bring to boiling; reduce heat. Simmer, covered, for 1 hour.

2 Add carrot. Return to boiling; reduce heat. Simmer, covered, for 7 minutes. Combine the cold water and cornstarch; add to pan along with rice. Cook and stir until slightly thickened. If desired, add wine; heat for 2 minutes more. Discard bay leaf.

3 To serve, ladle into soup bowls. If desired, garnish with herb sprigs.

Nutrition Facts per serving: 351 calories, 13 g total fat, 82 mg cholesterol, 914 mg sodium, 26 g carbohydrate, 32 g protein.

Caldo Gallego

Caldo is a Spanish word that means broth. *This broth-based soup has three kinds of meat to make it stick-to-the-ribs good.*

Prep: 30 minutes

Cook: 1 hour 35 minutes

Stand: 1 hour

Makes: 6 servings

1 cup dry navy or Great Northern beans

4 cups cold water

6 cups water

1 pound beef flank steak or boneless round steak, cut into large pieces

1 8-ounce smoked pork hock or meaty ham bone

1 2-ounce piece salt pork, rind removed (optional)

½ cup chopped onion

2 medium potatoes, peeled and cubed

1 medium green sweet pepper, chopped

1 3 ½-ounce package cooked smoked chorizo sausage links, sliced

4 ounces fresh turnip greens, stems removed and chopped (about 3 cups)

¼ teaspoon ground black pepper

1 Rinse beans. In a 4-quart Dutch oven, combine beans and the 4 cups cold water. Bring to boiling; reduce heat. Simmer, uncovered, for 2 minutes. Remove from heat. Cover and let stand for 1 hour. (Or, omit simmering; soak the beans in cold water overnight in a covered pan or a bowl in a cool place.) Drain and rinse beans in a colander.

2 In the same Dutch oven combine beans and the 6 cups water. Add steak, pork hock or ham bone, salt pork (if using), and onion. Bring to boiling; reduce heat. Simmer, covered, about 1¼ hours or until beans are nearly tender, stirring occasionally.

3 Remove steak, pork hock or ham bone, and salt pork; set aside. Add potatoes, green pepper, and chorizo slices to Dutch oven. Return to boiling; reduce heat. Simmer, covered, for 20 minutes more.

4 Meanwhile, shred or finely chop steak; remove meat from pork hock or ham bone and chop. Discard bone and salt pork. Add meat to Dutch oven along with the turnip greens and black pepper. Cover and cook for 10 minutes more or until greens are tender.

Nutrition Facts per serving: 368 calories, 13 g total fat, 47 mg cholesterol, 361 mg sodium, 34 g carbohydrate, 30 g protein.

The Ultimate Split Pea Soup

This version of one of the best winter-chill chasers around gets extra flavor from the beef shank and the sweet-nutty parsnips.

Prep: 20 minutes

Cook: 1 hour

Makes: 8 servings

1 pound dry split green peas

2 quarts water (8 cups)

½ pound beef shank

1 large onion, chopped (1 cup)

2 small carrots, peeled and coarsely chopped (⅔ cup)

2 small parsnips, peeled and coarsely chopped (⅔ cup)

3 cloves garlic, finely chopped

1 teaspoon salt

2 bay leaves

Carrot strips (optional)

1 Sort through dry peas and discard any pebbles or discolored peas. Rinse and drain peas; combine with other ingredients (except carrot strips) in a 4-quart Dutch oven. Bring to boiling; reduce heat. Simmer, covered, on low heat for 1 hour or until nearly smooth, stirring occasionally. Discard bay leaves. Remove shank bone before serving.

2 If desired, when cool enough to handle, cut the meat off the bone and chop into small pieces. Return meat to soup and heat through.

3 To serve, ladle into soup bowls. If desired, garnish with carrot strips.

Nutrition Facts per serving with meat: 235 calories, 1 g total fat, 7 mg cholesterol, 297 mg sodium, 40 g carbohydrate, 17 g protein.

Scotch Barley Broth

With a damp, cool climate, the Scots know a thing or two about warming soups. Enjoy this classic with a slice of crusty bread on a cold, rainy night.

Prep: 15 minutes

Cook: 1 hour

Makes: 4 or 5 servings

12 ounces lamb stew meat, cut into 1-inch cubes*

½ teaspoon freshly ground black pepper

1 tablespoon cooking oil

3 14½-ounce cans beef broth

1 12-ounce bottle dark beer

⅔ cup pearl barley or quick-cooking barley

1 large leek, halved lengthwise and sliced (about ½ cup)

1 large turnip, peeled and cut into ½-inch pieces (1 cup)

2 medium carrots, sliced ½ inch thick (1 cup)

2 tablespoons snipped fresh parsley

1 In a 4-quart Dutch oven cook lamb with pepper in hot oil for 5 minutes. Pour off fat; discard. Add broth and beer to meat in pan. Bring to boiling; add pearl barley, if using. Reduce heat. Simmer, covered, for 30 minutes.

2 Add leek, turnip, and carrots to mixture in pan. Return to boiling; reduce heat. Simmer, covered, about 30 minutes more or until tender. (If using quick-cooking barley, add it about 12 minutes before stew is finished.) Stir in parsley. Ladle into bowls.

*__Note:__ If desired, stew beef can be substituted for lamb.

Nutrition Facts per serving: 321 calories, 9 g total fat, 43 mg cholesterol, 1,089 mg sodium, 34 g carbohydrate, 22 g protein.

Winter Minestrone

This classic Italian soup features a harvest of vegetables—winter squash, potatoes, fennel, onion, and kale.

Prep: 30 minutes

Cook: 8 to 10 hours plus 5 minutes

Makes: 8 servings

1 pound uncooked Italian or pork sausage links, cut into ¾-inch slices

2½ cups peeled winter squash (such as butternut, acorn, hubbard, or turban) cut into 1-inch cubes

1½ cups peeled potatoes cut into 1-inch pieces

2 medium fennel bulbs, trimmed and cut into 1-inch pieces

1 15-ounce can red kidney beans, rinsed and drained

1 large onion, chopped

2 cloves garlic, minced

½ teaspoon dried sage, crushed

4 cups chicken broth or vegetable broth

1 cup dry white wine

4 cups chopped kale or fresh spinach

1 In a large skillet cook the sausage until brown. Drain off fat.

2 In a 5- to 6-quart electric crockery cooker place squash, potatoes, fennel, beans, onion, garlic, and sage. Top with sausage. Pour broth and wine over all.

3 Cover and cook on low-heat setting for 8 to 10 hours or on high-heat setting for 4 to 5 hours. Stir in kale or spinach. Cover; cook 5 minutes more.

Nutrition Facts per serving: 315 calories, 14 g total fat, 38 mg cholesterol, 933 mg sodium, 27 g carbohydrate, 16 g protein.

Smoked Sausage and Bean Soup

Kids and grownups alike will love this tasty soup. And the cook in the family will appreciate how easily it comes together—especially if you use packaged preshredded cabbage.

Start to Finish: 45 minutes

Makes: 6 servings

1 medium onion, finely chopped
  (½ cup)

1 teaspoon bottled minced garlic

2 tablespoons margarine or butter

6 cups water

2 medium potatoes, chopped
  (2 cups)

1 pound fully cooked smoked
  turkey sausage, sliced

1 15-ounce can red kidney beans,
  rinsed and drained

1 teaspoon instant beef bouillon
  granules

2 cups chopped cabbage or
  packaged shredded cabbage
  with carrot (coleslaw mix)

¼ cup tomato paste or catsup

3 tablespoons vinegar

1 In a 4-quart Dutch oven cook the onion and garlic in margarine or butter until tender but not brown. Add the water, potatoes, sausage, beans, and bouillon granules. Bring to boiling; reduce heat. Simmer, covered, for 15 minutes. Add the cabbage or coleslaw mix, tomato paste or catsup, and vinegar. Simmer, covered, 10 minutes more.

Nutrition Facts per serving: 298 calories, 13 g total fat, 51 mg cholesterol, 933 mg sodium, 30 g carbohydrate, 20 g protein.

Ham and Vegetable Soup

Here's a great way to use leftover holiday ham. It's also a great reason to keep some ham on hand so you can make this up anytime!

Prep: 20 minutes

Cook: 15 minutes

Makes: 5 servings

1 medium onion, chopped (½ cup)

2 cloves garlic, minced

1 tablespoon margarine or butter

5 cups water

6 ounces tiny new potatoes, cut into ¾-inch pieces (1¼ cups)

1 medium carrot, sliced (½ cup)

½ cup long grain rice

1½ teaspoons instant chicken bouillon granules

2 tablespoons snipped fresh dill or 1 teaspoon dried dill

¼ teaspoon ground white or black pepper

2 cups cooked reduced-sodium or regular ham, cubed (10 ounces)

½ of a 10-ounce package fresh spinach, stems removed and leaves chopped (about 3¼ cups, lightly packed)

1 cup light cream or half-and-half

Fresh dill (optional)

1 In a 4-quart Dutch oven cook onion and garlic in hot margarine or butter until tender. Add the water, potatoes, carrot, rice, bouillon granules, dried dill, if using, and pepper. Bring to boiling; reduce heat. Simmer, covered, for 15 minutes, or until rice and vegetables are just tender. Add ham, spinach, and fresh dill, if using. Simmer, covered, for 1 to 2 minutes more, just until spinach is wilted. Stir in cream or half-and-half; heat through, but do not boil.

2 To serve, ladle into soup bowls. If desired, garnish each serving with additional fresh dill.

Nutrition Facts per serving: 260 calories, 10 g total fat, 42 mg cholesterol, 960 mg sodium, 29 g carbohydrate, 15 g protein.

Lentil, Barley, and Ham Soup

Got a hungry houseful on your hands? This soup combines barley with lentils for a true stick-to-the-ribs soup. If you're watching your sodium intake, use lower-sodium ham.

Prep: 25 minutes

Cook: 50 minutes

Makes: 6 servings

¾ cup chopped onion

½ cup chopped celery

1 clove garlic, minced

2 tablespoons margarine or butter

½ cup brown lentils, rinsed and drained

5 cups water

1½ teaspoons snipped fresh oregano or ½ teaspoon dried oregano, crushed

1½ teaspoons snipped fresh basil or ½ teaspoon dried basil, crushed

¾ teaspoon snipped fresh rosemary or ¼ teaspoon dried rosemary, crushed

¼ teaspoon ground black pepper

1½ cups diced reduced-fat and reduced-sodium cooked ham

1 cup thinly sliced carrots

½ cup quick-cooking barley

1 14½-ounce can tomatoes, cut up

1 In a large saucepan cook the onion, celery, and garlic in hot margarine or butter until tender but not brown. Stir in the lentils, the water, oregano, basil, rosemary, and pepper. Bring to boiling; reduce heat. Simmer, covered, for 30 minutes.

2 Stir in the ham, carrots, and uncooked barley. Bring to boiling; reduce heat. Simmer, covered, about 20 minutes more or just until carrots are tender. Stir in the undrained tomatoes. Heat through.

Nutrition Facts per serving: 211 calories, 6 g total fat, 16 mg cholesterol, 602 mg sodium, 28 g carbohydrate, 13 g protein.

LOVE THOSE LENTILS!

Lentils are a popular ingredient in soups and stews. While red and yellow lentils are widely available, our recipes generally call for the brown lentil. More exotic varieties—green, white, or black—also can be found in specialty food stores.

   If you wish to substitute one type of lentil for another, you may need to adjust the cooking time specified in the recipe. For instance, red lentils are usually smaller than brown, which means you'd need to reduce cooking time significantly. In the case of yellow lentils, which are the same size as brown, cooking time should remain the same. Check package labels for instructions on cooking, whichever lentils you choose.

Chicken Soup with Lentils And Barley

Cook up this soup for a comforting Sunday night supper, and take leftovers to work for a satisfying lunch during the week. To use another variety of lentils, see tip on page 106.

Prep: 25 minutes

Cook: 40 minutes

Makes: 6 servings

1 cup sliced leeks or chopped onion

½ cup chopped red or green sweet pepper

1 clove garlic, minced

2 tablespoons margarine or butter

2 14½-ounce cans chicken broth

1½ cups water

½ cup brown lentils, rinsed and drained

½ teaspoon dried basil, crushed

¼ teaspoon dried oregano, crushed

¼ teaspoon dried rosemary, crushed

¼ teaspoon ground black pepper

1½ cups chopped cooked chicken or turkey

1½ cups sliced carrots

½ cup quick-cooking barley

1 14½-ounce can tomatoes, cut up

1 In a large saucepan cook leeks or onion, sweet pepper, and garlic in margarine or butter until tender. Carefully stir in broth, the water, lentils, basil, oregano, rosemary, and pepper. Bring to boiling; reduce heat. Cover and simmer for 20 minutes.

2 Stir in the chicken, carrots, and uncooked barley. Simmer, covered, about 20 minutes more or just until carrots are tender. Add the undrained tomatoes; heat through.

Nutrition Facts per serving: 292 calories, 8 g total fat, 34 mg cholesterol, 659 mg sodium, 34 g carbohydrate, 21 g protein.

Heavenly Hearty and Healthy Soup

With the help of your crockery cooker, you can have a luscious low-fat, low-calorie meal waiting when you get home.

Prep: 25 minutes

Cook: 6 hours

Makes: 4 to 6 servings

1 pound uncooked ground turkey

1 cup sliced celery

½ cup thinly sliced carrot

2½ cups tomato juice

1 14½-ounce can French-cut green beans, drained

1 cup fresh mushrooms, sliced ¼-inch thick

½ cup chopped tomato

1 tablespoon dried minced onion

1½ teaspoons Worcestershire sauce

1 teaspoon dried basil, crushed

1 teaspoon dried oregano, crushed

½ teaspoon garlic powder

½ teaspoon sugar

¼ teaspoon ground black pepper

1 bay leaf

1 In a large skillet, cook the turkey, celery, and carrot until turkey is brown. Drain off fat.

2 In a 3½- to 4-quart electric crockery cooker combine turkey mixture, tomato juice, green beans, mushrooms, tomato, dried minced onion, Worcestershire sauce, basil, oregano, garlic powder, sugar, black pepper, and bay leaf.

3 Cover and cook on low-heat setting for 6 hours or on high-heat setting for 2½ to 3 hours. Remove and discard bay leaf.

Nutrition Facts per serving: 245 calories, 10 g total fat, 90 mg cholesterol, 953 mg sodium, 17 g carbohydrate, 23 g protein.

Red Seafood Chowder

Use the pastry topper if you're feeling splashy (and have a little extra time)—but if you're feeling rushed, leave it off and top the soup with crackers or croutons instead.

Start to Finish: 45 minutes

Makes: 4 servings

½ cup chopped onion

½ cup chopped fennel (half of a medium fennel bulb); reserve leafy tops for garnish, if desired

1 tablespoon olive oil or cooking oil

4 medium tomatoes, peeled, seeded, and cut up (2 cups)

2 14½-ounce cans reduced-sodium chicken broth

¼ teaspoon curry powder

¼ teaspoon ground black pepper

12 ounces fresh bay scallops and/or peeled and deveined medium shrimp, and/or skinless fish fillets, such as red snapper or halibut, cut into bite-size pieces

½ of a 17¼-ounce package frozen puff pastry (1 sheet), thawed

Fennel tops (optional)

1 Preheat oven to 400°F. In a large saucepan cook onion and fennel in hot olive oil or cooking oil until tender but not brown. Stir in the tomatoes, chicken broth, curry powder, and pepper. Bring to boiling; reduce heat. Simmer, covered, for 15 minutes.

2 Add scallops and/or shrimp, and/or fish to saucepan. Return to boiling; reduce heat. Simmer, uncovered, for 2 to 3 minutes more or until scallops and/or shrimp are opaque, and fish flakes easily when tested with a fork.

3 Meanwhile, unfold pastry onto a floured surface. Cut into 8 squares, triangles, rounds, and/or other shapes with a sharp knife or cookie cutter. Place pieces on an ungreased baking sheet. Bake about 10 minutes or until golden brown and puffed.

4 To serve, ladle hot chowder into bowls. Top each with baked puff pastry. If desired, add fennel tops.

Nutrition Facts per serving: 431 calories, 24 g total fat, 28 mg cholesterol, 861 mg sodium, 34 g carbohydrate, 21 g protein.

Halibut Chowder with Spinach

This winning stew gets extra flavor from clam juice, leeks, and bacon, and added richness from half-and-half. If halibut is unavailable, substitute cod or orange roughy fillets.

Start to Finish: 45 minutes

Makes: 4 servings

1 pound fresh or frozen halibut steaks, cut ¾ inch thick

4 slices bacon, halved crosswise

2½ cups chopped, peeled potatoes

1 cup sliced leeks or chopped onion

1 8-ounce bottle clam juice

½ cup chicken broth

1½ teaspoons snipped fresh dill or ½ teaspoon dried dill

¼ teaspoon salt

¼ teaspoon ground white pepper

1½ cups half-and-half or light cream

1 cup milk

2 tablespoons all-purpose flour

3 cups chopped fresh spinach or ½ of a 10-ounce package frozen chopped spinach, thawed and well drained

1 Thaw halibut steaks, if frozen, and cut into ¾-inch cubes. Discard skin and bones. In a large saucepan cook bacon until crisp. Remove bacon, reserving 1 tablespoon drippings, if desired. Drain bacon on paper towels; crumble bacon and set aside.

2 In the same saucepan combine reserved bacon drippings, if desired, potatoes, leeks or onion, clam juice, chicken broth, dill, salt, and pepper. Bring to boiling; reduce heat. Simmer, covered, about 15 minutes or until potatoes are tender. With the back of a fork, mash potatoes slightly against the side of the pan.

3 Combine half-and-half, milk, and flour until smooth; add to potato mixture. Cook and stir just until mixture comes to boiling; add halibut. Reduce heat and simmer, uncovered, for 3 to 4 minutes or until fish flakes easily when tested with a fork. Stir in spinach. Cook 1 to 2 minutes more or just until spinach is wilted.

4 To serve, ladle soup into bowls. Sprinkle with crumbled bacon.

Nutrition Facts per serving: 431 calories, 18 g total fat, 80 mg cholesterol, 630 mg sodium, 33 g carbohydrate, 35 g protein.

Succotash Soup and Dumplings

Surprise! This satisfying soup with irresistible cornmeal dumplings is actually low in fat!

Start to Finish: 45 minutes

Makes: 4 servings

3 cups water

2 cups cut fresh corn or one
  10-ounce package frozen whole
  kernel corn

1 cup frozen lima beans

½ cup chopped celery

½ cup sliced carrot

½ cup chopped onion

1 tablespoon snipped fresh dill or
  ½ teaspoon dried dill

2 teaspoons instant vegetable
  bouillon granules

1 recipe Cornmeal Dumplings

⅓ cup packaged instant mashed
  potato flakes

1 In a large saucepan combine the 3 cups water, the corn, lima beans, celery, carrot, onion, dill, and bouillon granules. Bring to boiling; reduce heat. Simmer, covered, for 8 to 10 minutes or until the vegetables are almost tender.

2 Meanwhile, prepare Cornmeal Dumplings; set aside. Stir potato flakes into the soup. Cook and stir until slightly thickened and bubbly.

3 Drop the dumpling mixture from a tablespoon into 8 mounds directly on top of the bubbling soup. Cover tightly and simmer for 10 to 12 minutes (do not lift cover) or until a wooden toothpick inserted in a dumpling comes out clean.

4 To serve, ladle soup and dumplings into soup bowls.

Cornmeal Dumplings: In a medium saucepan combine 1 cup water, ⅓ cup yellow cornmeal, ¼ teaspoon salt, and dash ground black pepper. Cook and stir until thickened and bubbly. Remove from heat; cool slightly. Add 1 beaten egg, beating until smooth. In a small bowl stir together ⅔ cup all-purpose flour, 1 tablespoon grated Parmesan cheese, 1 tablespoon snipped fresh parsley, and 1 teaspoon baking powder. Stir into the cornmeal mixture with a fork just until moistened.

Nutrition Facts per serving: 279 calories, 3 g total fat, 55 mg cholesterol, 765 mg sodium, 55 g carbohydrate, 11 g protein.

The Best-Ever Minestrone

Kale and Swiss chard have been under-appreciated in American cooking. Here's a chance to enjoy them in a superior take on this classic Italian soup.

Prep: 20 minutes

Cook: 40 minutes

Makes: 8 servings

¼ cup olive oil

2 medium carrots, sliced (1 cup)

2 stalks celery, chopped (1 cup)

1 medium onion, chopped (½ cup)

1 small head savoy or green cabbage, coarsely shredded

6 leaves Swiss chard, coarsely shredded

6 leaves kale, coarsely shredded

8 ounces green beans, trimmed and cut into 2-inch pieces

8 ounces potatoes, peeled and cubed (optional)

8 cups chicken broth

2 14½-ounce cans tomatoes, cut up, or 3 cups chopped fresh tomatoes

½ teaspoon ground black pepper

2 15-ounce cans white kidney (cannellini) beans, rinsed and drained, or 1½ cups dry Great Northern beans, cooked*

1 medium zucchini or yellow summer squash, quartered lengthwise and sliced

¾ cup snipped fresh basil

1 In a 6- to 8-quart Dutch oven heat olive oil over medium-high heat. Add carrots, celery, and onion. Cook and stir for 2 minutes. Add cabbage, Swiss chard, and kale. Cook and stir vegetables about 6 minutes more or until greens are wilted. Add green beans and potatoes, if desired. Cook and stir for 2 minutes more.

2 Add chicken broth, undrained tomatoes, and pepper. Bring to boiling; reduce heat. Simmer, covered, for 20 minutes. Stir in white kidney or Great Northern beans, and zucchini or squash. Return to boiling; reduce heat. Simmer, covered, 20 minutes more. Stir in basil.

*Note: To cook dry beans, rinse beans. In a 4- to 5-quart Dutch oven combine rinsed beans and 5 cups cold water. Bring to boiling; reduce heat. Simmer, uncovered, for 2 minutes. Remove from heat. Cover and let stand for 1 hour. (Or omit simmering; soak dry beans in cold water overnight in a covered Dutch oven.) Drain beans and rinse. In the same pan combine rinsed beans and 5 cups fresh water. Bring to boiling; reduce heat. Cover and simmer beans for 1 to 1½ hours or until beans are tender, stirring occasionally.

Nutrition Facts per serving: 213 calories, 9 g total fat, 1 mg cholesterol, 1,159 mg sodium, 27 g carbohydrate, 14 g protein.

Spinach and Lentil Soup

Great lentil soups never fade away—they just get reinvented in a myriad of tasty renditions. This top-notch meatless version brings a windfall of colorful spinach to your table.

Prep: 20 minutes

Cook: 35 minutes

Makes: 4 servings

1 medium onion, chopped (½ cup)

2 cloves garlic, minced

1 tablespoon cooking oil

1 cup brown lentils, rinsed and drained

4 cups water

1 7½-ounce can tomatoes, cut up

4 teaspoons instant vegetable or chicken bouillon granules

1 tablespoon Worcestershire sauce

½ teaspoon salt

½ teaspoon dried thyme, crushed

¼ teaspoon fennel seeds, crushed

¼ teaspoon ground black pepper

1 bay leaf

2 medium carrots, chopped (1 cup)

1 10-ounce package frozen chopped spinach

1 tablespoon balsamic or red wine vinegar

1 In a large saucepan or Dutch oven cook onion and garlic in hot oil until tender but not brown. Stir in the lentils, the water, undrained tomatoes, bouillon granules, Worcestershire sauce, salt, thyme, fennel seeds, pepper, and bay leaf. Bring to boiling; reduce heat. Simmer, covered, for 20 minutes. Add carrots and frozen spinach. Bring to boiling, breaking up spinach with a fork; reduce heat. Simmer, covered, about 15 minutes more or until lentils are tender. Stir in vinegar. Discard bay leaf.

2 To serve, ladle soup into bowls.

Nutrition Facts per serving: 277 calories, 5 g total fat, 0 mg cholesterol, 1,751 mg sodium, 45 g carbohydrate, 18 g protein.

Potato-Bean Soup

Creamy cannellini beans and a variety of colorful vegetables make this a wholly satisfying recipe for those times when you feel like going meatless.

Prep: 20 minutes

Cook: 20 minutes

Makes: 4 to 6 servings

2 medium carrots, shredded (1 cup)

½ cup sliced celery

1 clove garlic, minced

2 teaspoons margarine, melted

4 cups chicken broth

3 medium potatoes, peeled and cut up (3 cups)

2 tablespoons snipped fresh dill or 2 teaspoons dried dill

1 15-ounce can white kidney (cannellini) beans or Great Northern beans, rinsed and drained

½ cup light dairy sour cream or plain nonfat yogurt

1 tablespoon all-purpose flour

⅛ teaspoon ground black pepper

Salt (optional)

1 In a large saucepan cook and stir carrots, celery, and garlic in hot margarine over medium heat for 4 minutes or until tender. Carefully stir in broth, potatoes, and dill. Bring to boiling; reduce heat. Simmer, covered, for 20 to 25 minutes or until potatoes are tender. With the back of a spoon, lightly mash about half of the potatoes in the broth. Add the beans to the potato mixture.

2 In a small bowl stir together sour cream or yogurt, flour, pepper, and, if desired, salt to taste; stir into potato mixture. Cook and stir until thickened and bubbly. Cook and stir 1 minute more.

Nutrition Facts per serving: 280 calories, 6 g total fat, 4 mg cholesterol, 1,035 mg sodium, 48 g carbohydrate, 16 g protein.

Italian Dutch Oven Chowder

This chowder makes a festive first course to a holiday dinner or a hearty and warming main-dish soup for any cold-weather evening.

Start to Finish: 45 minutes

Makes: 8 to 10 side-dish servings (or 6 main-dish servings)

4 slices bacon

2 large carrots, sliced ½ inch thick (1½ cups)

2 medium parsnips, sliced ½ inch thick, cutting larger pieces in half (1½ cups)

2 medium onions, cut into thin wedges

3 medium potatoes, chopped (3 cups)

2 14½-ounce cans reduced-sodium chicken broth

½ teaspoon garlic salt

¼ teaspoon ground black pepper

3 tablespoons margarine or butter, melted

3 tablespoons all-purpose flour

2 cups milk

2 cups frozen whole kernel corn

1 pint shucked oysters with juice (optional)

Snipped fresh chives or parsley (optional)

1 In a 4-quart Dutch oven cook bacon until crisp. Remove bacon, reserving 1 tablespoon drippings in the pan. Drain bacon on paper towels; crumble and set aside.

2 Add carrots, parsnips, and onions to Dutch oven. Cook over medium heat for 8 to 10 minutes or until brown, stirring occasionally.

3 Add potatoes, chicken broth, garlic salt, and pepper. Bring to boiling; reduce heat. Simmer, covered, about 15 minutes or until potatoes are tender.

4 In a small bowl stir together melted margarine or butter and flour. Stir flour-margarine mixture, milk, and corn into chowder in Dutch oven.

5 Cook and stir over medium heat until slightly thickened. If desired, add oysters and liquid to soup; cook until heated through and oysters curl around edges.

6 To serve, ladle into soup bowls. Sprinkle each serving with crumbled bacon and, if desired, chives or parsley.

Nutrition Facts per side-dish serving: 267 calories, 13 g total fat, 23 mg cholesterol, 566 mg sodium, 33 g carbohydrate, 7 g protein.

Root Veggie Soup with Curry Croutons

This meal-in-a-bowl takes advantage of winter's crop of tasty root vegetables. The curry croutons are easy to make and add an extra spark of flavor.

Prep: 25 minutes
Cook: 25 minutes
Bake: 15 minutes
Makes: 4 servings

1 medium fennel bulb (4 to 5 ounces)

¼ cup chopped onion

1 clove garlic, minced

2 teaspoons cooking oil

3 cups chicken broth

1 medium turnip, peeled and cubed (about ¾ cup)

1 small potato, peeled and cubed (about ⅔ cup)

1 medium carrot, sliced (½ cup)

¼ teaspoon ground white or black pepper

1 tablespoon olive oil

½ teaspoon curry powder

3 ¾-inch slices Italian bread, torn into bite-size pieces

1 15-ounce can white kidney (cannellini) beans, rinsed and drained

¼ cup half-and-half or light cream

Salt

1 Cut off and discard upper stalks of fennel, snipping and reserving feathery leaves for garnish. Wash fennel bulb; finely chop. In a large saucepan cook onion and garlic in hot cooking oil about 5 minutes or until onion is tender. Carefully add chopped fennel, broth, turnip, potato, carrot, and pepper. Bring to boiling; reduce heat. Simmer, covered, for 25 to 30 minutes or until vegetables are very tender. Cool slightly.

2 Meanwhile, preheat oven to 350°F. In a medium bowl combine olive oil and curry powder. Add torn bread pieces; toss until coated. Spread bread in a single layer in a 15×10×1-inch baking pan. Bake 15 to 20 minutes or until croutons begin to brown, stirring once.

3 Place one-third of the vegetable mixture in a blender container or food processor bowl.* Cover and blend or process until smooth; pour into a medium bowl. Repeat with remaining mixture. Return all to saucepan. Stir in beans and half-and-half or light cream; heat through. Season to taste with salt.

4 To serve, ladle into soup bowls. Garnish with croutons and, if desired, snipped fennel tops.

*Note: For information on blending and pureeing soups, see page 5.

Nutrition Facts per serving: 282 calories, 10 g total fat, 6 mg cholesterol, 935 mg sodium, 42 g carbohydrate, 14 g protein.

Carbonnade of Beef and Vegetables, **recipe page 134**

With these hearty
one-bowl meals, all
you need to add is a
loaf of crusty bread
and a side salad for
a bountiful meal.

Comforting Stews

Allspice Meatball Stew

Frozen meatballs are one of the best suppertime shortcut tricks—and this quick and hearty stew is an all-time great way to use them.

Start to Finish: 30 minutes

Makes: 8 servings

1 16-ounce package frozen prepared Italian-style meatballs

3 cups green beans, cut into 2-inch pieces or 3 cups frozen cut green beans

2 cups packaged peeled baby carrots

1 14½-ounce can beef broth

2 teaspoons Worcestershire sauce

½ to ¾ teaspoon ground allspice

½ teaspoon ground cinnamon

2 14½-ounce cans stewed tomatoes

1 In a Dutch oven combine the meatballs, green beans, carrots, beef broth, Worcestershire sauce, allspice, and cinnamon. Bring to boiling; reduce heat. Simmer, covered, for 10 minutes.

2 Stir in undrained tomatoes. Return to boiling; reduce heat. Simmer, covered, about 5 minutes more or until vegetables are crisp-tender.

Note: This soup freezes well. Freeze 1-, 2-, or 4-serving portions in sealed freezer containers. To reheat, place frozen soup in a large saucepan. Heat, covered, over medium heat about 30 minutes, stirring occasionally to break apart.

Nutrition Facts per serving: 233 calories, 13 g total fat, 37 mg cholesterol, 938 mg sodium, 18 g carbohydrate, 12 g protein.

Oxtail Ragoût

No, this recipe doesn't truly call for a tail of an ox—most "oxtails" today actually hail from beef or veal. The cut brings a distinctive richness to the stew.

Prep: 30 minutes

Cook: 1½ hours

Makes: 5 or 6 servings

2 tablespoons cooking oil

1 pound oxtails, cut into 1½- to 2-inch pieces (optional)

1 pound boneless beef short ribs (if omitting oxtails, use an additional 4 ounces boneless beef short ribs

2 14½-ounce cans beef broth (about 3½ cups)

½ cup dry red wine or beef broth

½ cup coarsely chopped shallots

4 cloves garlic, minced

2 bay leaves

½ teaspoon salt

¼ to ½ teaspoon coarsely ground black pepper

1 pound carrots, peeled and cut into ¾-inch pieces

1 pound rutabagas or turnips, peeled and cut into ¾-inch cubes

1 cup coarsely chopped onion

⅓ cup all-purpose flour

⅓ cup snipped fresh parsley

Hot cooked couscous or Israeli couscous (optional)

1 In a 4- to 6-quart Dutch oven heat cooking oil. Brown oxtails and short ribs on all sides in hot oil. Drain fat. To avoid spattering, carefully add beef broth, wine, shallots, garlic, bay leaves, salt, and coarsely ground black pepper to meat in pan. Bring to boiling; reduce heat. Simmer, covered, about 1 hour or until meat is nearly tender.

2 Add carrots, rutabagas, and onion to meat mixture in pan. Return to boiling; reduce heat. Simmer, covered, for 30 to 45 minutes more or until meat and vegetables are tender. Discard bay leaves. Remove meat; allow to cool slightly.

3 Meanwhile, in a small bowl stir ⅓ cup cold water into the flour until smooth (or shake together in a screw-top jar). Stir into pan. Cook and stir until thickened and bubbly. Cook and stir for 1 minute more. Cut meat into bite-size pieces, discarding any bones. Return meat to pan; heat through. Stir in snipped parsley. If desired, season to taste with additional salt and pepper and serve meat and vegetables over hot cooked couscous.

Nutrition Facts per serving: 441 calories, 27 g total fat, 53 mg cholesterol, 881 mg sodium, 28 g carbohydrate, 18 g protein.

Carbonnade of Beef and Vegetables

Beef and beer are hallmarks of this age-old Belgian stew. The recipe gets its name from a French word that refers to a meat dish that's cooked over flames or coals.

Prep: 25 minutes

Cook: 1 hour 20 minutes

Makes: 8 servings

2 pounds boneless beef top round steak, cut into 1-inch cubes

2 tablespoons cooking oil

3 large leeks or medium onions, sliced

2 12-ounce cans or bottles light beer (3 cups)

¼ cup red wine vinegar

3 tablespoons brown sugar

2 tablespoons instant beef bouillon granules

4 cloves garlic, minced

2 bay leaves

2 teaspoons dried thyme, crushed

2 teaspoons Worcestershire sauce

½ teaspoon ground black pepper

1 pound carrots

4 parsnips

¼ cup water

2 tablespoons quick-cooking tapioca

Hot cooked wide noodles

1 In a 4½-quart Dutch oven brown the meat, half at a time, in hot oil. Drain off fat. Return all meat to Dutch oven. Add leek or onion slices, beer, vinegar, brown sugar, bouillon granules, garlic, bay leaves, thyme, Worcestershire sauce, and pepper. Bring mixture to boiling; reduce heat. Simmer, covered, for 45 minutes, stirring occasionally. Peel and cut carrots and parsnips into ½-inch diagonal slices; add to Dutch oven. Cook, covered, for 35 to 40 minutes more or until meat and vegetables are tender.

2 Discard bay leaves; skim any fat from the sauce. Combine the water and tapioca. Stir tapioca mixture into the meat mixture; cook and stir over medium heat until thickened and bubbly. Cook and stir for 2 minutes more. Serve over hot noodles.

Nutrition Facts per serving: 337 calories, 9 g total fat, 72 mg cholesterol, 762 mg sodium, 30 g carbohydrate, 30 g protein.

Beef Stew with Sour Cream Biscuits

Stews can sometimes be a high-fat indulgence. This recipe achieves greatness because some of its savory flavor comes from light sour cream. Simply draining the meat can help keep the fat content in check as well.

Prep: 30 minutes

Bake: 1 hour 50 minutes

Makes: 6 servings

¾ **pound boneless beef top round steak, cut into ½-inch cubes**

1 **tablespoon all-purpose flour**

Nonstick cooking spray

1 **cup chopped onion**

3 **medium potatoes, cubed (3 cups)**

1 **14½-ounce can Italian-style stewed tomatoes**

½ **of a 6-ounce can low-sodium tomato paste (⅓ cup)**

2½ **cups water**

2 **teaspoons instant beef bouillon granules**

1 **tablespoon sugar**

1 **teaspoon dried thyme, crushed**

1 **teaspoon Worcestershire sauce**

1 **bay leaf**

1 **cup cubed eggplant, peeled, if desired**

1 **recipe Sour Cream Biscuits**

⅓ **cup light dairy sour cream**

1 **tablespoon all-purpose flour**

2 **teaspoons milk**

1 **teaspoon sesame seeds (optional)**

Fresh thyme sprigs (optional)

1 In a plastic bag combine meat and the 1 tablespoon flour; shake to coat meat. Spray an unheated 4½-quart Dutch oven with nonstick cooking spray. Add meat and onion; cook until meat is brown and onion is tender. Drain off any fat. Add potatoes, undrained tomatoes, tomato paste, the water, bouillon granules, sugar, thyme, Worcestershire sauce, and bay leaf. Bake, covered, in a 350°F oven for 1 hour. Add eggplant. Cover and bake for 30 minutes more.

2 Meanwhile, prepare Sour Cream Biscuits. Remove stew from oven; increase oven temperature to 425°F. Discard bay leaf. Combine sour cream and remaining 1 tablespoon flour; stir into stew. Brush biscuits with milk. If desired, sprinkle biscuits with sesame seeds.

3 Arrange cutout biscuits on meat mixture. Bake, uncovered, for 20 to 25 minutes or until biscuits are golden.

4 To serve, ladle stew and biscuits into soup bowls. If desired, garnish each serving with fresh thyme.

Sour Cream Biscuits: In a large mixing bowl stir together 1¼ cups all-purpose flour and 1½ teaspoons baking powder. Cut in ¼ cup margarine or butter until mixture resembles coarse crumbs. Stir in ⅓ cup light dairy sour cream and ¼ cup nonfat milk. On a lightly floured surface knead dough 8 to 10 times. Roll or pat to ½-inch thickness. With a 2-inch biscuit cutter, cut dough into circles. Makes 12 biscuits.

Nutrition Facts per serving: 408 calories, 13 g total fat, 40 mg cholesterol, 757 mg sodium, 53 g carbohydrate, 22 g protein.

Ginger and Molasses Beef Stew

Slightly sweet, yet savory, this veggie-packed stew makes enough for a crowd.

Prep: 35 minutes

Cook: 9 hours plus 30 minutes

Makes: 8 servings

2 pounds lean beef stew meat, cut
   into 1-inch cubes

1 tablespoon cooking oil

4 carrots, thickly sliced

2 medium parsnips, thickly sliced

1 large onion, sliced

1 stalk celery, sliced

1 ¼-inch slice fresh ginger or
   ½ teaspoon ground ginger

¼ cup quick-cooking tapioca

1 14½-ounce can diced tomatoes

¼ cup vinegar

¼ cup molasses

1 teaspoon salt

½ teaspoon ground black pepper

½ cup raisins

1 In a large skillet cook meat, a third at a time, in hot oil until brown. Drain off fat.

2 In a 3½-, 4-, or 5-quart electric crockery cooker place carrots, parsnips, onion, celery, and, if using, fresh ginger. Sprinkle tapioca over vegetables. Add meat. In a medium bowl combine undrained tomatoes, vinegar, molasses, salt, black pepper, and, if using, ground ginger; pour over all.

3 Cover and cook on low-heat setting for 9 to 10 hours or on high-heat setting for 4 to 5 hours. Stir in raisins. Cover and cook for 30 minutes more. If using, remove fresh ginger before serving.

Nutrition Facts per serving: 564 calories, 19 g total fat, 110 mg cholesterol, 962 mg sodium, 58 g carbohydrate, 40 g protein.

Cassoulet-Style Stew

Cassoulet is a French stew that often requires lots of work. This quicker version offers many of the satisfying hallmarks of the original—lamb, beans, and vegetables—but doesn't take all day to make! Serve it alongside a crisp green salad tossed with a garlic vinaigrette.

Prep: 50 minutes

Stand: 1 hour

Cook: 1¾ hours

Makes: 12 servings

6 cups water

1 pound dry navy beans, rinsed and drained

1 meaty lamb shank (1 to 1½ pounds)

1 tablespoon olive oil or cooking oil

2 cups chopped celery (including leaves)

2 medium potatoes, coarsely chopped (2 cups)

¾ cup coarsely chopped carrot

¾ cup coarsely chopped parsnip

3 cloves garlic, minced

7 cups water

8 ounces fresh mushrooms, sliced (3 cups)

1¼ cups dry black-eyed peas, rinsed and drained

½ cup dry red wine or beef broth

2 teaspoons salt

½ teaspoon ground black pepper

1 28-ounce can diced tomatoes

2 tablespoons snipped fresh thyme

1 tablespoon snipped fresh rosemary

Fresh rosemary sprigs (optional)

1 In a large saucepan combine the 6 cups water and the beans. Bring to boiling; reduce heat. Simmer, uncovered, for 2 minutes. Remove from heat. Cover and let stand for 1 hour. Drain and rinse beans.

2 In an 8- to 10-quart Dutch oven brown lamb shank in hot oil. Add celery, potatoes, carrot, parsnip, and garlic. Cook over medium-high heat for 5 minutes, stirring frequently. Add the 7 cups water, the mushrooms, black-eyed peas, wine or broth, salt, pepper, and drained beans. Bring to boiling; reduce heat. Simmer, covered, about 1½ hours or until the beans and peas are tender. Remove lamb shank.

3 Add the undrained tomatoes, thyme, and snipped rosemary to bean mixture. When cool enough to handle, remove meat from bone; discard bone. Chop meat; add to bean mixture. Bring to boiling; reduce heat. Simmer, covered, for 15 minutes more.

4 To serve, ladle into soup bowls. If desired, garnish each serving with fresh rosemary sprigs.

Nutrition Facts per serving: 287 calories, 4 g total fat, 14 mg cholesterol, 553 mg sodium, 46 g carbohydrate, 18 g protein.

Fruited Lamb Stew and Mashed Sweet Potatoes

Today's bistros often serve hearty stews paired with mashed potatoes. This recipe taps into the trend and takes it a step further, with colorful, flavor-packed mashed sweet potatoes.

Prep: 30 minutes

Cook: 1½ hours

Makes: 6 servings

2 pounds lamb stew meat, cut into 1-inch cubes

¼ teaspoon salt

¼ teaspoon ground black pepper

2 tablespoons cooking oil

2 tablespoons all-purpose flour

2 14½-ounce cans vegetable broth

1 12-ounce can apricot or mango nectar

1 2-inch stick cinnamon or ¼ teaspoon ground cinnamon

3 cloves garlic, minced

½ teaspoon ground cumin

½ teaspoon ground cardamom

⅛ teaspoon thread saffron, crushed

3 medium carrots, cut into ½-inch pieces (1½ cups)

1½ cups frozen pearl onions

1 cup dried apricots

1 cup dried pitted plums (prunes)

1 recipe Mashed Sweet Potatoes

Fresh sage leaves (optional)

1 Season lamb with salt and pepper. In a 4-quart Dutch oven brown meat, half at a time, in hot oil over medium-high heat. Drain off excess oil. Return all meat to pan. Sprinkle meat with flour, stirring to coat. Add vegetable broth, nectar, cinnamon, garlic, cumin, cardamom, and saffron; stir to combine. Bring to boiling; reduce heat. Simmer, covered, for 1 hour or until meat is nearly tender.

2 Add carrots, onions, apricots, and plums. Return to boiling; reduce heat. Simmer, covered, about 30 minutes more or until vegetables are tender. Remove stick cinnamon, if using. Serve over Mashed Sweet Potatoes or your favorite mashed potatoes. If desired, garnish with sage leaves.

Mashed Sweet Potatoes: Peel and quarter 2 pounds sweet potatoes. In a large saucepan, cook potatoes, covered, in a moderate amount of boiling, lightly salted water for 20 to 25 minutes or until tender; drain. Mash with a potato masher or beat with an electric mixer on low speed. Add ¼ cup margarine or butter, cut up, and ¼ cup plain yogurt; beat or mash until smooth. If necessary, stir in a little low-fat or nonfat milk to create the desired consistency. Serve with stew.

Nutrition Facts per serving: 613 calories, 20 g total fat, 97 mg cholesterol, 881 mg sodium, 80 g carbohydrate, 36 g protein.

Sausage Stew Pot

Fully cooked Polish sausage and no-hassle lentils cook together quickly and add up to a lively one-dish meal that's great for a busy weeknight.

Prep: 25 minutes

Cook: 15 minutes

Makes: 5 servings

1 pound fully cooked Polish sausage, halved lengthwise and sliced

8 ounces fresh mushrooms, sliced (3 cups)

1 large onion, halved and sliced

1 medium yellow, red, or green sweet pepper, cut into strips (1 cup)

1 clove garlic, minced

1 tablespoon cooking oil

4 cups water

2 cups shredded cabbage

1 cup brown lentils, rinsed and drained

2 tablespoons rice vinegar

1 tablespoon brown sugar

2 teaspoons instant chicken bouillon granules

1/8 teaspoon ground black pepper

1 In a 4-quart Dutch oven cook the sausage, mushrooms, onion, sweet pepper strips, and garlic in hot oil about 5 minutes or just until vegetables are tender. Add the water, cabbage, lentils, vinegar, brown sugar, bouillon granules, and black pepper. Bring to boiling; reduce heat. Simmer, covered, for 15 to 20 minutes or until vegetables and lentils are tender.

Nutrition Facts per serving: 399 calories, 32 g total fat, 61 mg cholesterol, 1,281 mg sodium, 17 g carbohydrate, 16 g protein.

Pork and Mushroom Stew

Spend just a little time putting this on the stove, then you can relax and enjoy yourself, knowing that a wholesome stew supper is simmering to perfection.

Prep: 25 minutes

Cook: 1 hour

Makes: 4 servings

1 pound pork stew meat, cut into 1-inch cubes

2 tablespoons margarine or butter

1 10½-ounce can condensed chicken broth

¼ cup dry white wine

3 tablespoons snipped fresh parsley

¾ teaspoon snipped fresh thyme or ¼ teaspoon dried thyme, crushed

¼ teaspoon garlic powder

⅛ teaspoon ground black pepper

1 bay leaf

2 cups frozen whole small onions

1 10-ounce package frozen tiny whole carrots

1 4-ounce can whole mushrooms, drained

¾ cup cold water

¼ cup all-purpose flour

1 tablespoon lemon juice

1 In a large saucepan brown pork, half at a time, in margarine or butter. Return all meat to pan. Stir in the chicken broth, wine, parsley, thyme, garlic powder, pepper, and bay leaf. Bring to boiling. Reduce heat and simmer, covered, for 40 minutes.

2 Add the frozen onions, frozen carrots, and mushrooms. Return to boiling. Reduce heat and simmer, covered, about 15 minutes more or until vegetables are tender. Discard bay leaf.

3 Combine the cold water and flour; add to stew with lemon juice. Cook and stir until thickened and bubbly. Cook and stir for 1 minute more.

Nutrition Facts per serving: 361 calories, 18 g total fat, 74 mg cholesterol, 800 mg sodium, 20 g carbohydrate, 26 g protein.

Pork and Squash Stew

Ward off winter's chill with this delicately sweet fix-and-forget stew.

Prep: 25 minutes

Cook: 7 hours

Makes: 4 to 5 servings

1½ **pounds boneless pork shoulder roast, cut into 1-inch cubes**

2 **tablespoons cooking oil**

1½ **pounds winter squash (such as hubbard, butternut, or acorn), peeled and cut into 1-inch pieces**

1 **medium onion, sliced**

½ **cup dried apricots**

2 **tablespoons raisins**

3 **tablespoons instant flour (Wondra) or** ¼ **cup instant mashed potato flakes**

2 **tablespoons brown sugar**

½ **teaspoon ground cinnamon**

¼ **teaspoon salt**

¼ **teaspoon ground nutmeg**

⅛ **teaspoon ground ginger**

1¼ **cups chicken broth**

1 **tablespoon bottled steak sauce**

1 In a large skillet cook meat, half at a time, in hot oil about 5 minutes or until brown. Drain off fat.

2 In a 3½- to 4-quart electric crockery cooker place squash, onion, apricots, and raisins. Add meat. Sprinkle with flour or potato flakes, brown sugar, cinnamon, salt, nutmeg, and ginger. Combine chicken broth and steak sauce; pour over all.

3 Cover and cook on low-heat setting for 7 hours or on high-heat setting for 3½ hours. Stir gently before serving.

Nutrition Facts per serving: 474 calories, 21 g total fat, 115 mg cholesterol, 647 mg sodium, 35 g carbohydrate, 37 g protein.

Brunswick Stew

This beloved Southern stew, which hails from Brunswick County, Virginia, was traditionally served at barbecues. You'll love its delicious, down-home appeal.

Start to Finish: 1¼ hours

Makes: 4 or 5 servings

2 pounds meaty chicken pieces, skinned*

2 smoked pork hocks (12 to 16 ounces each)

3 medium onions, cut into thin wedges

1 14½-ounce can diced tomatoes

½ cup chicken broth

4 cloves garlic, minced

1 tablespoon Worcestershire sauce

1 teaspoon dry mustard

1 teaspoon dried thyme, crushed

¼ teaspoon ground black pepper

¼ teaspoon bottled hot pepper sauce

2 cups loose-pack frozen cut okra

1 cup loose-pack frozen baby lima beans

1 cup loose-pack frozen whole kernel corn

¼ cup cold water

2 tablespoons all-purpose flour

Salt (optional)

Ground black pepper (optional)

1 In a large Dutch oven combine the chicken pieces, pork hocks, onions, undrained tomatoes, chicken broth, garlic, Worcestershire sauce, mustard, thyme, the ¼ teaspoon black pepper, and hot pepper sauce. Bring to boiling; reduce heat. Simmer, covered, for 35 to 45 minutes or until chicken is no longer pink (170°F for breasts; 180°F for thighs and drumsticks). Remove pork hocks (and chicken, if desired); cool slightly.

2 Cut meat from hocks; chop meat and set aside, discarding bone. (Cut chicken into bite-size pieces, if desired.) Add okra, lima beans, and corn to mixture in Dutch oven. Return to boiling; reduce heat. Simmer, covered, for 10 to 15 minutes more or just until vegetables are tender.

3 In a small bowl stir the cold water into all-purpose flour until smooth (or shake together in a screw-top jar). Stir into stew. Cook and stir until thickened and bubbly; cook and stir for 1 minute more. Stir in meat from pork hocks (and chicken, if cut up). If desired, season to taste with salt and black pepper.

***Note:** If desired, brown the chicken pieces before cooking. Heat 2 tablespoons cooking oil in the Dutch oven. Add the chicken pieces and cook over medium heat about 15 minutes, turning to brown the chicken evenly. Drain off fat. Continue as directed.

Nutrition Facts per serving: 454 calories, 10 g total fat, 109 mg cholesterol, 794 mg sodium, 44 g carbohydrate, 48 g protein.

Chicken Stew with Tortellini

Easy to use but so very tasty, tortellini has to be one of the best convenience products around—and this recipe takes full advantage of this time-saver.

Start to Finish: 35 minutes

Makes: 6 servings

2 cups water

1 14½-ounce can reduced-sodium chicken broth

1 medium yellow summer squash

6 cups torn beet greens, turnip greens, or spinach

1 green sweet pepper, coarsely chopped (¾ cup)

1 cup dried cheese-filled tortellini

1 medium onion, cut into thin wedges

1½ cups sliced carrots

1½ teaspoons snipped fresh rosemary

½ teaspoon salt-free seasoning blend

¼ teaspoon ground black pepper

2 cups chopped cooked chicken

1 tablespoon snipped fresh basil

1 In a Dutch oven bring the water and chicken broth to boiling. Meanwhile, halve summer squash lengthwise and cut into ½-inch slices. Add squash, greens, sweet pepper, tortellini, onion, carrots, rosemary, seasoning blend, and black pepper to Dutch oven.

2 Return to boiling; reduce heat. Simmer, covered, about 15 minutes or until pasta and vegetables are nearly tender.

3 Stir in chicken. Cook, covered, about 5 minutes more or until pasta and vegetables are tender. Stir in basil.

Nutrition Facts per serving: 234 calories, 6 g total fat, 45 mg cholesterol, 530 mg sodium, 22 g carbohydrate, 22 g protein.

Classic Chicken-Sausage Gumbo

Here's a delicious and filling version of a traditional Louisiana gumbo. It starts—as all good gumbos must—with a rich roux to thicken and flavor the dish.

Prep: 30 minutes

Cook: 15 minutes

Makes: 4 servings

⅓ **cup all-purpose flour**

¼ **cup cooking oil**

½ **cup chopped onion**

½ **cup chopped celery**

½ **cup chopped green sweet pepper**

4 **cloves garlic, minced**

¼ **teaspoon ground black pepper**

¼ **teaspoon ground red pepper**

3 **cups chicken broth, heated**

1½ **cups chopped cooked chicken or turkey**

8 **ounces andouille sausage or fully cooked smoked sausage links, halved lengthwise and cut into ½-inch slices**

1½ **cups sliced okra or one 10-ounce package frozen cut okra**

2 **bay leaves**

3 **cups hot cooked rice**

Filé powder (optional)*

1 For roux, in a large heavy saucepan or Dutch oven combine flour and oil until smooth. Cook over medium-high heat for 5 minutes, stirring constantly. Reduce heat to medium. Cook and stir about 15 minutes or until roux is dark reddish brown.

2 Stir in onion, celery, sweet pepper, garlic, black pepper, and ground red pepper. Cook over medium heat for 3 to 5 minutes or just until vegetables are crisp-tender, stirring often.

3 Gradually stir in hot chicken broth, chicken or turkey, sausage, okra, and bay leaves. Bring to boiling. Reduce heat and simmer, covered, about 15 minutes or until okra is tender. Discard bay leaves. Serve in bowls with rice. If desired, serve with ¼ to ½ teaspoon filé powder to stir into each serving.

***Note:** Filé (fee LAY) powder is ground sassafras leaves that Cajun cooks use to thicken and add a thymelike flavor to gumbos. Because it gets stringy when it's boiled, pass it at the table and let each person add his or her own.

Nutrition Facts per serving: 614 calories, 24 g total fat, 87 mg cholesterol, 1,129 mg sodium, 61 g carbohydrate, 37 g protein.

Simple Chicken Stew

This recipe is great for days when you want a hearty stew supper—but you're off to a late start! It comes together in just 35 minutes and offers a simmered-all-day satisfaction.

Start to Finish: 35 minutes

Makes: 5 servings

1 cup chopped onion

1 clove garlic, minced

1 tablespoon cooking oil

1 cup thinly sliced carrots

¾ cup chicken broth

2 tablespoons catsup

⅛ teaspoon ground nutmeg

⅛ teaspoon ground black pepper

1½ cups milk

4 teaspoons cornstarch

2 cups chopped cooked chicken

1 cup frozen peas, thawed

½ cup whipping cream

½ cup grated Parmesan cheese

2½ cups hot cooked rice

Fresh parsley sprigs (optional)

1 In a saucepan cook onion and garlic in hot oil until tender. Add carrots, broth, catsup, nutmeg, and pepper. Bring to boiling; reduce heat. Simmer, covered, for 5 minutes. Stir together milk and cornstarch until smooth. Add milk mixture to broth mixture. Cook and stir until thickened and bubbly; cook and stir for 2 minutes more. Stir in chicken, peas, cream, and cheese; heat through. Serve over rice. If desired, garnish with fresh parsley.

Nutrition Facts per serving: 470 calories, 21 g total fat, 100 mg cholesterol, 521 mg sodium, 40 g carbohydrate, 29 g protein.

Root Cellar Bouillabaisse

You don't need hours to simmer this version of bouillabaisse. It's fast, easy, and brimming with sensational fish and seafood.

Start to Finish: 25 minutes

Makes: 6 servings

12 ounces fresh or frozen firm
  white-flesh fish (such as cod,
  haddock, or grouper)

8 fresh or frozen cleaned baby
  clams and/or fresh or frozen
  mussels in shells

4 ounces fresh or frozen peeled
  and deveined shrimp with tails

2 medium onions, sliced and
  separated into rings

1 teaspoon bottled minced garlic or
  2 cloves garlic, minced

2 tablespoons olive oil

2 cups chicken broth or clam juice

1 cup dry white wine or
  chicken broth

1 14½-ounce can stewed tomatoes,
  cut up

1 teaspoon finely shredded orange
  peel

1 teaspoon dried thyme, crushed

1 teaspoon fennel seeds

½ teaspoon salt

½ teaspoon ground black pepper

⅛ teaspoon ground saffron

1 7-ounce can sweet potatoes,
  drained and cut up

6 slices French bread, toasted
  (optional)

1 Thaw fish and seafood, if frozen. Cut fish into 1½-inch pieces.

2 In a large saucepan cook the onions and garlic in hot oil about 3 minutes or just until tender, stirring frequently. Add the 2 cups broth or clam juice, the wine or broth, undrained tomatoes, orange peel, thyme, fennel seeds, salt, black pepper, and saffron. Bring to boiling; add seafood and fish. Return to boiling; reduce heat. Simmer, covered, for 3 to 5 minutes or until shrimp turns opaque and fish flakes easily when tested with a fork. Add sweet potatoes; heat through, stirring gently.

3 To serve, remove and discard clams or mussels that have not opened. If desired, ladle soup into bowls over French bread. Makes 6 servings.

Nutrition Facts per serving: 334 calories, 7 g total fat, 61 mg cholesterol, 889 mg sodium, 40 g carbohydrate, 22 g protein.

Eggplant and White Bean Stew

This elegant eggplant stew can be made with any variety of eggplant you like—white, green, or purple. You can search Asian markets for exotic varieties, such as Japanese and Thai.

Start to Finish: 25 minutes

Makes: 4 servings

2 cloves garlic, minced

1 tablespoon olive oil

1 medium onion, cut into thin
   wedges (½ cup)

1 pound eggplant, any type, peeled
   and cut into ¾-inch cubes (4 to
   5 cups)

2 14½-ounce cans vegetable broth
   or reduced-sodium chicken
   broth

1 15-ounce can navy, white kidney
   (cannellini), or Great Northern
   beans, rinsed and drained

3 tablespoons tomato paste

2 teaspoons snipped fresh
   marjoram or ½ teaspoon dried
   marjoram, crushed

⅛ teaspoon ground black pepper

2 tablespoons snipped fresh
   parsley

   Fresh marjoram sprigs (optional)

1 In a large saucepan cook and stir garlic in hot olive oil over medium-high heat for 30 seconds. Add onion. Cook and stir for 2 minutes. Add eggplant. Cook and stir 3 minutes more.

2 Stir in vegetable or chicken broth, beans, tomato paste, marjoram, and pepper. Bring to boiling; reduce heat. Simmer, covered, for 5 minutes or just until eggplant is tender. Do not overcook.

3 To serve, ladle into serving bowls. Sprinkle with parsley. If desired, garnish with marjoram.

Nutrition Facts per serving: 199 calories, 5 g total fat, 0 mg cholesterol, 1,342 mg sodium, 36 g carbohydrate, 10 g protein.

Winter Vegetable Stew

Take your pick—if you have a clay pot cooker, use it. If not, this recipe can be made in a Dutch oven. Either way, it's a wonderful veggie-mushroom medley your family will love. Note: Be sure to allow time to properly soak the clay pot before using.

Prep: 45 minutes

Bake: 1¾ hours

Makes: 6 servings

- 1 large onion, chopped (1 cup)
- 2 tablespoons olive oil
- ¼ cup snipped fresh parsley
- ½ teaspoon dried sage, crushed
- ½ teaspoon dried thyme, crushed
- ¼ teaspoon dried rosemary, crushed
- 2 bay leaves
- 1 15-ounce can whole tomatoes, cut up
- ¼ cup dry red wine
- 2 tablespoons soy sauce
- 4 cloves garlic, minced
- 4 large parsnips (1 to 1½ pounds), peeled and cut into 2-inch pieces (3 to 4 cups)
- 2 large leeks (white parts only), halved lengthwise and cut into 1-inch pieces (1 cup)
- 2 14½-ounce cans Great Northern or navy beans, rinsed and drained
- 2 medium turnips, peeled and cut into wedges (1½ cups)
- 4 ounce shiitake, cremini, brown or button mushrooms, halved (1½ cups)
- 2 small potatoes, quartered (about 1½ cups)

1 Do not preheat the oven when using a clay pot. Submerge top and bottom of a 2 to 3 quart clay pot (unglazed) in a sink of cool water; allow to soak 30 minutes.

2 In a saucepan cook onion in hot oil over medium-high heat for 12 to 15 minutes or until onions are tender and golden, stirring occasionally. Stir in the parsley, sage, thyme, rosemary, and bay leaves. Add undrained tomatoes, wine, soy sauce, and garlic.

3 Drain the clay pot. Fill with parsnips, leeks, drained beans, turnip wedges, mushrooms, and potatoes (there should be about 10 cups of vegetables). Pour tomato mixture over the vegetables. Put top on clay pot and place in cold oven.

4 Set oven temperature to 350°F and bake for 1¾ to 2 hours or until vegetables are tender. Discard bay leaves. If desired, season to taste with salt and black pepper and garnish with additional chopped fresh parsley and fresh sage leaves.

To prepare in a Dutch oven: In a large ovenproof pan cook onion in hot oil over medium-high heat for 12 to 15 minutes or until the onions are tender and golden, stirring occasionally. Stir in ¼ cup parsley, dried sage, thyme, rosemary, and bay leaves. Add undrained tomatoes, wine, soy sauce, and garlic. Add parsnips, leeks, turnips, and potatoes to the pan. Cover; bake in a 350°F oven for 1 hour. Stir in beans and mushrooms. Bake, covered, about 15 minutes more or until vegetables are tender. Discard bay leaves. Continue as directed.

Nutrition Facts per serving: 304 calories, 6 g total fat, 0 mg cholesterol, 515 mg sodium, 54 g carbohydrate, 12 g protein.

Bean and Squash Chili, **recipe page 192**

When the cold wind blows, take comfort in these creative takes on the classic winter warmer.

Best-Ever Chili Recipes

Fruit and Nut Chili

This recipe includes a traditional mix of tomatoes, kidney beans, and ground beef, but a blend of unique spices, plus apples and almonds, steer it into gourmet territory.

Prep: 35 minutes
Cook: 1 hour 10 minutes
Makes: 8 servings

1½ pounds lean ground beef

4 medium onions, chopped (2 cups)

3 cloves garlic, minced

2 14½-ounce cans tomatoes, cut up

1 15-ounce can tomato sauce

1 14½-ounce can chicken broth

3 medium green, red, and/or yellow sweet peppers, chopped (2¼ cups)

2 4-ounce cans diced green chile peppers, drained

2 cooking apples (such as Granny Smith or Jonathan), cored and chopped (about 2 cups)

3 tablespoons chili powder

2 tablespoons unsweetened cocoa powder

1 tablespoon curry powder

1 teaspoon ground cinnamon

1 15-ounce can red kidney beans, rinsed and drained

⅔ cup slivered almonds

Raisins, cheddar cheese, and plain yogurt or dairy sour cream (optional)

1 In a large Dutch oven cook beef, onions, and garlic until meat is brown. Drain off fat.

2 Stir in undrained tomatoes, tomato sauce, broth, sweet peppers, green chile peppers, apples, chili powder, cocoa powder, curry, and cinnamon. Bring to boiling; reduce heat. Simmer, covered, for 1 hour, stirring occasionally.

3 Add kidney beans and almonds. Heat through. If desired, serve with raisins, cheddar cheese, and yogurt or sour cream.

Nutrition Facts per serving: 330 calories, 15 g total fat, 54 mg cholesterol, 1,097 mg sodium, 31 g carbohydrate, 25 g protein.

Indo-Texan Curry Chili

If you're a fan of Indian or Thai food, then sign up for this chili! Curry powder, coconut milk, and lemon peel bring exciting flavor dimensions found in both cuisines to one savory bowl.

Prep: 20 minutes

Cook: 1½ hours

Makes: 6 servings

2 pounds coarsely ground beef

4 cloves garlic, minced

1 tablespoon hot Madras curry powder, salt-free curry seasoning blend, or curry powder

2 teaspoons ground coriander

1 teaspoon ground cumin

1 teaspoon finely shredded lemon peel

2 cups chopped red sweet peppers

1 15-ounce can tomato puree

2 10-ounce cans diced tomatoes and green chile peppers

1 10½-ounce can condensed beef broth

1 cup canned unsweetened coconut milk

¼ cup catsup

Hot cooked rice

Snipped fresh basil (optional)

Chopped peanuts, raisins, and/or chutney (optional)

1 In a 4-quart Dutch oven cook ground beef and garlic until meat is brown. Drain fat. Stir in curry powder, coriander, cumin, and lemon peel. Stir in sweet peppers, tomato puree, undrained tomatoes, broth, coconut milk, and catsup. Bring to boiling; reduce heat. Simmer, uncovered, for 1½ hours or until desired consistency.

2 To serve, ladle chili into bowls over hot cooked rice. If desired, garnish each serving with snipped basil and serve with peanuts, raisins, and/or chutney.

Nutrition Facts per serving: 511 calories, 23 g total fat, 95 mg cholesterol, 923 mg sodium, 42 g carbohydrate, 34 g protein.

Black Bean Chili

This recipe calls on many of the hallmarks of a classic chili, but black beans give it just enough of that "off-the-beaten-path" touch to put it into the "all-time-great" category.

Prep: 15 minutes
Cook: 20 minutes
Makes: 4 servings

¾ **pound ground beef**

¾ **cup sliced green onions**

1 **small green or red sweet pepper, chopped (½ cup)**

⅓ **cup coarsely shredded carrot**

1 **14½-ounce can low-sodium tomatoes, cut up**

1 **15-ounce can black beans, rinsed and drained**

2 **8-ounce cans low-sodium tomato sauce**

2 **jalapeño or serrano chile peppers, seeded and chopped (see tip, page 176)**

1½ **to 2 teaspoons chili powder**

¼ **teaspoon ground black pepper**

Shredded cheddar cheese (optional)

Fresh basil leaves (optional)

Salt

Ground black pepper

1 In a 3-quart saucepan cook ground beef, onions, sweet pepper, and carrot until meat is brown. Drain fat. Stir in undrained tomatoes, black beans, tomato sauce, jalapeño peppers, chili powder, and black pepper. Bring to boiling; reduce heat. Simmer, covered, for 20 minutes. Season to taste with salt and black pepper.

2 To serve, ladle into bowls. If desired, top with cheese and basil.

Nutrition Facts per serving: 311 calories, 11 g total fat, 53 mg cholesterol, 367 mg sodium, 31 g carbohydrate, 26 g protein.

Italian Chili

Hot cooked rice helps to capture all the delicious juices of this Italian meal-in-a-bowl.

Prep: 20 minutes

Cook: 6 hours

Makes: 6 to 8 servings

1 pound lean ground beef

½ pound bulk Italian sausage

1 cup chopped onion

1 cup chopped green sweet pepper

3 cloves garlic, minced

1 28-ounce can Italian-style tomatoes, cut up

1 15-ounce can chickpeas (garbanzo beans), rinsed and drained

1 15-ounce can light red kidney beans, rinsed and drained

1 cup water

3 tablespoons Worcestershire sauce

2 to 3 tablespoons chili powder

2 teaspoons dried basil, crushed

2 teaspoons dried oregano, crushed

½ teaspoon bottled hot pepper sauce (optional)

¼ teaspoon salt

Hot cooked rice (optional)

Shredded cheddar cheese (optional)

1 In a large skillet cook ground beef, sausage, onion, green pepper, and garlic until meat is brown and vegetables are tender. Drain off fat.

2 In a 3½- or 4-quart electric crockery cooker combine the meat mixture, undrained tomatoes, chickpeas, beans, the water, Worcestershire sauce, chili powder, basil, oregano, bottled hot pepper sauce (if desired), and salt.

3 Cover and cook on low-heat setting for 6 to 8 hours or cook on high-heat setting for 3 to 4 hours. If desired, serve over hot cooked rice and top with cheese.

Nutrition Facts per serving: 436 calories, 20 g total fat, 72 mg cholesterol, 992 mg sodium, 36 g carbohydrate, 29 g protein.

Chili with Double-Bean Toss

Serve this gutsy chili Texas-style—with the Double-Bean Toss on the side. Or, if you'd rather, stir the bean mixture in.

Prep: 25 minutes

Cook: 10 hours

Makes: 6 servings

1 pound boneless beef top round steak, cut into ³⁄₄-inch pieces

1 tablespoon cooking oil

2 14¹⁄₂-ounce cans diced tomatoes

1 14-ounce can beef broth

1 cup chopped onion

1 or 2 fresh jalapeño or serrano peppers (see tip, page 176), finely chopped

2 cloves garlic, minced

4 teaspoons chili powder

1 tablespoon brown sugar

1¹⁄₂ teaspoons dried oregano, crushed

¹⁄₂ teaspoon ground cumin

¹⁄₄ teaspoon ground black pepper

1 recipe Double-Bean Toss (optional)

Dairy sour cream (optional)

Fresh cilantro or parsley leaves (optional)

Tortilla chips (optional)

1 In a large skillet cook meat, half at a time, in 1 tablespoon hot oil until brown. Drain off fat.

2 In a 3¹⁄₂- or 4-quart electric crockery cooker combine undrained tomatoes, broth, onion, jalapeño or serrano peppers, the 2 cloves garlic, the chili powder, brown sugar, oregano, cumin, and black pepper. Stir in meat.

3 Cover and cook on low-heat setting for 10 to 12 hours or on high-heat setting for 5 to 6 hours.

4 If desired, serve the chili with Double-Bean Toss. If desired, top with sour cream and garnish with fresh cilantro or parsley and tortilla chips.

Nutrition Facts per serving: 200 calories, 8 g total fat, 45 mg cholesterol, 511 mg sodium, 13 g carbohydrate, 18 g protein.

Double-Bean Toss: In a bowl combine one 15-ounce can pinto beans, rinsed and drained; one 15-ounce can black beans, rinsed and drained; ¹⁄₂ teaspoon finely shredded lime peel; 1 tablespoon lime juice; 1 tablespoon cooking oil; and 1 clove garlic, minced. Toss to mix

Texas-Style Bowls of Red

Texas is known for foods with a hot-and-spicy kick. Enjoy this taste of the Lone Star state.

Prep: 25 minutes

Cook: 1¼ hours

Makes: 6 servings

20 small dried hot chile peppers
(see tip, at right) or
2 tablespoons crushed
red pepper

2 dried ancho peppers (see tip, at
right) or 2 tablespoons chili
powder

¾ pound beef round steak, cut into
½-inch cubes

¾ pound boneless pork, cut into
½-inch cubes

2 tablespoons cooking oil

1 cup chopped onion

3 cloves garlic, minced

1 tablespoon ground cumin

½ teaspoon paprika

¼ teaspoon ground black pepper

1 14½-ounce can beef broth

1 12-ounce can or bottle beer

3 cups hot cooked pinto beans
and/or hot cooked rice

Sliced jalapeño chile peppers
(optional) (see tip, at right)

1 Crush hot chile peppers, if using. Remove stems and seeds from ancho peppers, if using; cut into 1-inch pieces. Put hot peppers and ancho peppers into a blender container or food processor bowl. Cover and blend or process until ground. Let pepper dust settle before opening blender or food processor. (If using crushed red pepper and chili powder, stir them together.) Set aside.

2 In a large saucepan or Dutch oven cook half of the meat in hot oil until brown. Remove meat and set aside. Add remaining meat, onion, garlic, cumin, paprika, black pepper, and ground chile pepper mixture (or the crushed red pepper and chili powder mixture, if using). Cook until meat is brown. Return all meat to saucepan. Stir in beef broth and beer. Bring to boiling. Reduce heat and simmer, covered, for 45 minutes. Uncover and simmer about 30 minutes more or until meat is tender and sauce is desired consistency, stirring occasionally. Serve with hot cooked pinto beans and/or rice. If desired, garnish with sliced jalapeño peppers.

Nutrition Facts per serving: 340 calories, 10 g total fat, 44 mg cholesterol, 445 mg sodium, 34 g carbohydrate, 26 g protein.

HANDLING HOT CHILE PEPPERS

Some of our recipes call for hot chile peppers, such as jalapeños. Because hot chile peppers contain volatile oils that can burn your skin and eyes, avoid direct contact with chiles as much as possible. When working with chile peppers, wear plastic or rubber gloves. If your bare hands do touch the chile peppers, wash your hands well with soap and water.

Chunky Chipotle Pork Chili

Chipotle peppers are jalapeño peppers that have been smoked. They come packed in adobo sauce—and they bring just the right amount of smoky heat to this dynamite pork chili.

Start to Finish: 25 minutes

Makes: 4 servings

1 small onion, chopped (⅓ cup)

4 cloves garlic, minced

2 teaspoons cooking oil

12 ounces well-trimmed pork tenderloin, cut into ¾-inch cubes

2 teaspoons chili powder

2 teaspoons ground cumin

1 medium yellow or red sweet pepper, cut into ½-inch chunks (¾ cup)

1 cup beer or beef broth

½ cup picante sauce or salsa

1 to 2 tablespoons finely chopped chipotle peppers in adobo sauce (see tip, page 176)

1 15-ounce can red or pinto beans, rinsed and drained

½ cup fat-free or light dairy sour cream

¼ cup snipped fresh cilantro

1 In a large saucepan cook onion and garlic in hot oil over medium-high heat about 3 minutes or until tender. Toss pork with chili powder and cumin; add to saucepan. Cook and stir until pork is browned, about 3 minutes. Add sweet pepper, beer or beef broth, picante sauce or salsa, and chipotle peppers; bring to boiling. Simmer, uncovered, about 5 minutes or just until pork is tender. Add beans; heat through.

2 To serve, ladle into bowls; top with sour cream and cilantro.

Nutrition Facts per serving: 286 calories, 5 g total fat, 60 mg cholesterol, 778 mg sodium, 31 g carbohydrate, 27 g protein.

Cincinnati-Style Chicken Chili

Cincinnati is famous for chili parlors, where diners often enjoy chili served over pasta.

Prep: 20 minutes

Cook: 55 minutes

Makes: 4 servings

1 pound uncooked ground chicken

1 large onion, chopped (1 cup)

1 clove garlic, minced

3 tablespoons chili powder

2 teaspoons paprika

1 teaspoon ground cumin

½ teaspoon salt

½ teaspoon ground cinnamon

⅛ teaspoon ground cloves

⅛ teaspoon ground red pepper

1 bay leaf

1 14½-ounce can stewed tomatoes

1 8-ounce can tomato sauce

½ cup water

1 tablespoon red wine vinegar

1 tablespoon molasses

1 15-ounce can kidney beans

Hot cooked spaghetti

1 In a 4½-quart Dutch oven cook ground chicken, onion, and garlic over medium heat for 5 to 7 minutes or until chicken is no longer pink. Drain off fat, if necessary.

2 Add chili powder, paprika, cumin, salt, cinnamon, cloves, red pepper, and bay leaf. Cook and stir over medium heat for 3 minutes more. Stir in undrained stewed tomatoes, tomato sauce, the water, red wine vinegar, and molasses. Bring to boiling; reduce heat. Simmer, covered, for 45 minutes, stirring occasionally.

3 Uncover and simmer to desired consistency. Discard bay leaf. In a medium saucepan heat undrained kidney beans; drain.

4 To serve, spoon sauce and beans over hot spaghetti.

Nutrition Facts per serving: 402 calories, 8 g total fat, 54 mg cholesterol, 1,223 mg sodium, 61 g carbohydrate, 30 g protein.

Chicken Chili with Rice

Once you discover the wonderfully fresh flavor that tomatillos add to recipes, you'll want to use them any way you can. Add this recipe to your tomatillo repertoire!

Start to Finish: 35 minutes

Makes: 4 servings

3 cloves garlic, minced

1 fresh jalapeño pepper, seeded and finely chopped (see tip, page 176)

1 tablespoon cooking oil

2 cups frozen small whole onions

1 cup reduced-sodium chicken broth or chicken broth

2 teaspoons chili powder

1 teaspoon ground cumin

1 teaspoon dried oregano, crushed

¼ teaspoon salt

⅛ teaspoon ground white pepper

⅛ teaspoon ground red pepper

1 19-ounce can white kidney (cannellini) beans, rinsed and drained

1 cup chopped cooked chicken

1 cup chopped tomatillos

2 cups hot cooked rice or couscous

1 In a large saucepan cook the garlic and jalapeño pepper in hot oil for 30 seconds. Carefully stir in onions, chicken broth, chili powder, cumin, oregano, salt, white pepper, and red pepper.

2 Bring to boiling; reduce heat. Simmer, covered, for 20 minutes. Add beans, chicken, and tomatillos; cook and stir until heated through. Serve over rice.

Nutrition Facts per serving: 335 calories, 8 g total fat, 34 mg cholesterol, 417 mg sodium, 51 g carbohydrate, 23 g protein.

Chili Blanc

White beans, ground turkey, and the absence of tomatoes make this chili live up to its name. Plenty of flavor from just the right seasonings makes it live up to the promise of an "all-time great" recipe.

Prep: 20 minutes

Cook: 25 minutes

Makes: 4 servings

12 ounces uncooked ground turkey

½ cup chopped onion

1 12-ounce can or bottle beer

½ cup water

2 to 4 medium jalapeño chile peppers, seeded and finely chopped (see tip, page 176)

2 teaspoons instant chicken bouillon granules

1½ teaspoons chili powder

1 teaspoon ground cumin

2 15-ounce cans Great Northern or two 15- or 19-ounce cans white kidney (cannellini) beans, rinsed and drained

1 tablespoon lime juice

Dairy sour cream (optional)

Fresh cilantro or parsley sprigs (optional)

Lime wedges (optional)

Chili powder (optional)

Bottled hot pepper sauce (optional)

1 In a large saucepan cook turkey and onion until turkey is no longer pink and onion is tender. Drain fat from pan, if necessary.

2 Stir in beer, the water, jalapeño peppers, bouillon granules, chili powder, and cumin. Bring mixture to boiling; reduce heat. Simmer, uncovered, for 20 minutes, stirring occasionally. Stir in the drained beans and lime juice. Cook 5 minutes more.

3 If desired, mash half of the beans to thicken chili; stir.

4 To serve, ladle into bowls. If desired, garnish with sour cream, cilantro or parsley, and lime wedges, and sprinkle with additional chili powder. If desired, pass pepper sauce.

Nutrition Facts per serving: 280 calories, 7 g total fat, 32 mg cholesterol, 818 mg sodium, 35 g carbohydrate, 24 g protein.

Turkey and Wild Rice Chili

You won't miss the beef—wild rice adds extra heartiness to this white-style chili

Prep: 20 minutes

Cook: 45 minutes

Makes: 8 to 10 servings

1 pound skinless, boneless turkey
   or chicken breast, cut into
   ½-inch pieces

1 tablespoon cooking oil

¼ cup chopped onion

1 clove garlic, minced

3 cups water

1 14½-ounce can chicken broth

⅔ cup wild rice, rinsed and drained

2 4-ounce cans diced green chile
   peppers

2 teaspoons chili powder

1 teaspoon ground cumin

1 15¼-ounce can whole kernel
   corn, drained

1 15-ounce can Great Northern
   beans, rinsed and drained

Bottled hot pepper sauce

Shredded Monterey Jack cheese

Dairy sour cream

Snipped fresh parsley (optional)

1 In a large saucepan or small Dutch oven, cook turkey or chicken, half at a time, in hot oil until brown, Remove from saucepan with a slotted spoon. Add onion and garlic to saucepan; cook until tender. Return turkey to saucepan.

2 Stir in the water, broth, wild rice, undrained chile peppers, chili powder, and cumin. Bring to boiling; reduce heat. Simmer, covered, for 35 to 40 minutes or until wild rice is tender. Stir in corn and beans. Heat through. Season to taste with several dashes of bottled hot pepper sauce.

3 To serve, ladle into soup bowls. Serve with cheese and sour cream. If desired, garnish with parsley.

Nutrition Facts per serving: 314 calories, 11 g total fat, 55 mg cholesterol, 542 mg sodium, 32 g carbohydrate, 25 g protein.

Vegetable Chili with Cheese Topping

A cheddar and cream cheese topping provides a soothing counterpoint to this spicy chili. A little cocoa powder complements and deepens the flavors of the other ingredients.

Prep: 20 minutes

Cook: 45 minutes

Makes: 6 servings

Nonstick cooking spray

1¼ cups finely chopped zucchini

¾ cup finely chopped carrot

2 tablespoons chopped green onion

2 cloves garlic, minced

2 15-ounce cans hot-style chili beans in chili sauce

2 14½-ounce cans diced tomatoes

¼ cup catsup

1 tablespoon unsweetened cocoa powder

1 teaspoon chili powder

1 teaspoon ground cumin

1 teaspoon bottled hot pepper sauce

¼ teaspoon dried oregano, crushed

Salt

Ground black pepper

½ of an 8-ounce tub cream cheese with chive and onion

2 tablespoons milk

½ cup shredded cheddar cheese (2 ounces)

Green onion strips (optional)

1 Spray an unheated large saucepan with cooking spray. Cook zucchini, carrot, chopped green onion, and garlic in saucepan over medium heat for 2 minutes. Add undrained chili beans, undrained tomatoes, catsup, cocoa powder, chili powder, cumin, hot pepper sauce, and oregano. Bring to boiling; reduce heat. Simmer, uncovered, about 45 minutes or until desired consistency, stirring occasionally. Season to taste with salt and black pepper.

2 Meanwhile, in a small bowl stir together cream cheese and milk until smooth. Stir in cheddar cheese.

3 To serve, ladle chili into bowls. Spoon some of the cream cheese mixture onto each serving. If desired, garnish with green onion strips.

Nutrition Facts per serving: 281 calories, 13 g total fat, 30 mg cholesterol, 1,183 mg sodium, 39 g carbohydrate, 13 g protein.

Southwestern Bean Chili with Cornmeal Dumplings

If you've never made dumplings before, you're missing out on some true home-style goodness. This easy recipe is a great way to try your hand at making the chewy gems.

Prep: 30 minutes

Cook: 22 minutes

Makes: 6 servings

3 cups water

1 15-ounce can red kidney beans, rinsed and drained

1 15-ounce can black beans, pinto beans, or Great Northern beans, rinsed and drained

1 14½-ounce can Mexican-style stewed tomatoes

1 10-ounce package frozen whole kernel corn

1 cup sliced carrot

1 cup chopped onion

1 4-ounce can diced green chile peppers

2 tablespoons instant beef or chicken bouillon granules

1 to 2 teaspoons chili powder

2 cloves garlic, minced

⅓ cup all-purpose flour

¼ cup yellow cornmeal

1 teaspoon baking powder

Dash salt

Dash ground black pepper

1 beaten egg white

2 tablespoons milk

1 tablespoon cooking oil

1 In a 4-quart Dutch oven combine the water, kidney beans, black beans, undrained tomatoes, corn, carrot, onion, undrained chile peppers, bouillon granules, chili powder, and garlic. Bring to boiling. Reduce heat and simmer, covered, for 10 minutes.

2 Meanwhile, for dumplings, in a medium bowl stir together flour, cornmeal, baking powder, salt, and black pepper. In a small bowl combine egg white, milk, and oil. Add to flour mixture; stir with a fork just until combined. Drop dumpling mixture into 6 mounds on the bubbling chili. Simmer, covered, for 12 to 15 minutes or until a toothpick inserted in the dumplings comes out clean. (Do not lift lid while dumplings are cooking.)

3 To serve, ladle chili and dumplings into soup bowls.

Nutrition Facts per serving: 270 calories, 3 g total fat, 1 mg cholesterol, 1,593 mg sodium, 54 g carbohydrate, 15 g protein.

Bean and Squash Chili

You'll love the extra dimension of color and flavor that squash and corn bring to this quick-fixin' chili. Not a squash fan? Substitute carrots—they'll bring plenty of color to the mix too.

Prep: 10 minutes

Cook: 15 minutes

Makes: 4 servings

2 cups water

1 cup butternut squash, peeled, seeded, and cut into ½-inch cubes, or carrot, cut into ¼-inch slices

1 15-ounce can black beans or red kidney beans, rinsed and drained

1 14½-ounce can Mexican-style stewed tomatoes

1 cup frozen or canned baby corn, cut crosswise into ½-inch-long pieces

1 small onion, sliced and separated into rings

¼ cup tomato paste

1 vegetable bouillon cube

1 to 2 teaspoons chili powder

¾ teaspoon dried oregano, crushed

1 clove garlic, minced

Dairy sour cream (optional)

1 In a 3-quart saucepan combine the water and squash or carrots. Bring to boiling; reduce heat. Simmer, covered, for 5 minutes. Add beans, undrained tomatoes, corn, onion, tomato paste, bouillon cube, chili powder, oregano, and garlic. Bring to boiling; reduce heat. Simmer, covered, for 10 to 15 minutes.

2 To serve, ladle chili into soup bowls. If desired, top each serving with sour cream.

Nutrition Facts per serving: 163 calories, 1 g total fat, 0 mg cholesterol, 785 mg sodium, 36 g carbohydrate, 11 g protein.

Creamy Clam-Scallop Chowder, **recipe page 214**

Impress guests—while making the evening easy on yourself—with this selection of festive dinner-party fare.

Company-Special
Soups
& Stews

Country French Beef Stew

Light a fire in the fireplace and team this thick stew with some crusty country-style bread and a crisp green salad for a warming and memorable French-style supper.

Stand: 1 hour
Prep: 30 minutes
Cook: 1 hour 55 minutes
Makes: 6 servings

½ cup dry navy beans or one 15-ounce can white beans, rinsed and drained

4 cups water

¼ cup all-purpose flour

½ teaspoon ground black pepper

2 pounds boneless beef chuck pot roast, cut into 1-inch pieces

3 tablespoons olive oil

1 medium onion, cut into thin wedges

3 cloves garlic, minced

⅔ cup dry red wine

1¾ cups Beef Broth (see recipe, page 6) or one 14½-ounce can beef broth

1 cup chopped tomato

2 teaspoons dried thyme, crushed, or 2 tablespoons snipped fresh thyme

4 medium carrots, cut into ½-inch slices (2 cups)

2 medium parsnips, cut into ½-inch slices (1½ cups)

Snipped fresh thyme (optional)

1 If using dry beans, rinse beans. In a large saucepan combine drained beans and the 4 cups water. Bring to boiling; reduce heat. Simmer, uncovered, for 2 minutes. Remove from heat. Cover and let stand for 1 hour. (Or place beans in water in pan. Cover and let soak in a cool place for 6 to 8 hours or overnight.) Drain and rinse beans.

2 Place flour and pepper in a plastic bag. Add beef pieces, a few at a time, shaking to coat. In a 4- to 6-quart Dutch oven brown half of the beef in 1 tablespoon of the hot oil; remove beef. Add remaining oil, remaining beef, onion, and garlic to Dutch oven. Cook until beef is brown and onion is tender. Drain fat, if necessary. Stir in wine, scraping until the brown bits are dissolved. Return all beef to Dutch oven. Stir in the soaked dry beans (if using), broth, tomato, and dried thyme (if using). Bring to boiling; reduce heat. Simmer, covered, for 1½ hours.

3 Add carrots and parsnips. Return to boiling; reduce heat. Simmer, covered, for 25 to 30 minutes more or until beef and vegetables are tender. Add canned beans (if using); heat through. Stir in fresh thyme (if using). If desired, garnish with thyme.

Nutrition Facts per serving: 554 calories, 31 g total fat, 99 mg cholesterol, 295 mg sodium, 29 g carbohydrate, 34 g protein.

White Bean Soup with Sausage and Kale

There's a lot to love about this soup: White beans and mild Italian sausage bring a Tuscan influence, and frilly, deeply flavored kale leaves add a striking color and savory cabbagelike flavor. It's also one of the easiest company-special soups around!

Start to Finish: 35 minutes

Makes: 5 servings

12 ounces fresh mild Italian sausage links, pricked with a fork

¼ cup water

1 medium onion, chopped (1 cup)

2 cloves garlic, minced

1 tablespoon cooking oil

2 15-ounce cans white kidney (cannellini) beans, rinsed and drained

2 14½-ounce cans reduced-sodium chicken broth

1 cup seeded and coarsely chopped plum tomatoes (3 or 4 tomatoes)

1½ teaspoons snipped fresh marjoram or ½ teaspoon dried marjoram, crushed

7½ cups kale or spinach, coarsely chopped (10 to 12 ounces)

Ground black pepper (optional)

1 In a large skillet combine sausage and the water. Bring to boiling; reduce heat. Simmer, covered, about 15 minutes or until sausage is no longer pink. Uncover and cook about 5 minutes more or until sausage is brown, turning frequently. Remove sausage; cut into ¼- to ⅜-inch slices.

2 Meanwhile, in a large saucepan cook onion and garlic in hot oil about 5 minutes or until onion is tender. Stir in beans, broth, tomatoes, and dried marjoram (if using). Bring to boiling; reduce heat. Simmer, covered, for 15 minutes.

3 Stir in cooked sausage, kale or spinach, and fresh marjoram (if using). Simmer about 5 minutes more or until kale or spinach is tender. Season to taste with black pepper.

Nutrition Facts per serving: 282 calories, 11 g total fat, 39 mg cholesterol, 1,202 mg sodium, 31 g carbohydrate, 23 g protein.

Caribbean-Style Pork Stew

Hosting a lively crowd? This festive stew will keep the joint hopping!

Start to Finish: 30 minutes

Makes: 6 servings

1 15-ounce can black beans, rinsed
   and drained

1 14½-ounce can beef broth

1¾ cups water

12 ounces cooked lean boneless
   pork, cut into bite-size strips

3 plantains, peeled and cubed*

1 cup chopped tomatoes

½ of a 16-ounce package (2 cups)
   frozen pepper stir-fry
   vegetables (such as yellow,
   green, and red sweet peppers
   and onion)

1 tablespoon grated fresh ginger

1 teaspoon ground cumin

¼ teaspoon crushed red pepper

¼ teaspoon salt

3 cups hot cooked rice

   Crushed red pepper (optional)

   Fresh pineapple slices (optional)

1 In a Dutch oven combine beans, broth, and the water; heat to boiling.

2 Add the pork, plantains, and tomatoes to the bean mixture. Stir in the frozen vegetables, ginger, cumin, the ¼ teaspoon crushed red pepper, and the salt. Return mixture to boiling; reduce heat. Simmer, covered, for 10 minutes or until plantains are tender.

3 To serve, ladle soup into bowls. Serve with hot rice. If desired, sprinkle with additional crushed red pepper and garnish with pineapple.

***Note:** The flavor of a plantain will depend on the ripeness. A ripe, black-skinned plantain tastes like a banana. An almost-ripe, yellow plantain tastes similar to sweet potatoes. Unripe green plantains taste starchy but lose the starchy flavor upon cooking.

Nutrition Facts per serving: 425 calories, 9 g total fat, 52 mg cholesterol, 547 mg sodium, 66 g carbohydrate, 26 g protein.

Paella Soup

Paella is a traditional Spanish dish that's often made with chicken, meat, seafood, and rice. This recipe transforms the favorite into an easy entrée that's perfect casual dinner-party fare.

Start to Finish: 35 minutes

Makes: 4 servings

½ cup thinly sliced green onions

⅓ cup chopped red sweet pepper

1 clove garlic, minced

1 teaspoon cooking oil

1 14½-ounce can reduced-sodium chicken broth

½ cup uncooked long grain rice

1 bay leaf

¼ teaspoon salt

⅛ teaspoon ground red pepper

⅛ teaspoon ground turmeric

8 ounces cooked pork, cut into ¾-inch cubes

8 ounces peeled and deveined fresh shrimp

1 cup frozen peas

2 teaspoons snipped fresh oregano

1 In a large saucepan cook green onions, sweet pepper, and garlic in hot oil for 2 minutes.

2 Stir in chicken broth, rice, bay leaf, salt, red pepper, and turmeric. Bring to boiling; reduce heat. Simmer, covered, for 15 minutes. Stir in the cooked pork, shrimp, and peas. Simmer, covered, for 3 to 5 minutes more or until shrimp are opaque. Discard bay leaf. Stir in fresh oregano.

Nutrition Facts per serving: 324 calories, 10 g total fat, 139 mg cholesterol, 879 mg sodium, 25 g carbohydrate, 31 g protein.

Chicken Soup with Ham and Orzo

The smoky flavor of ham and the tangy bite of Swiss chard make this version of chicken noodle soup a cut above the rest.

Start to Finish: 35 minutes

Makes: 6 servings

2 chicken breast halves (about
  1 pound total)

4 14½-ounce cans reduced-sodium
  chicken broth

6 ounces dried orzo (rosamarina)

12 ounces fresh asparagus, trimmed
  and bias-sliced into 1½-inch
  pieces

4 cups lightly packed, thinly sliced
  Swiss chard leaves

4 plum tomatoes, seeded and
  chopped

2 ounces cooked boneless ham, cut
  into ½-inch pieces

Salt

Ground black pepper

Snipped fresh chives

Snipped fresh flat-leaf parsley

1 In a 4-quart Dutch oven combine chicken and broth. Bring to boiling; reduce heat. Simmer, covered, 20 minutes or until chicken is tender and no longer pink. Remove chicken from broth; cool chicken slightly.

2 Return broth to boiling; add orzo. Return to boiling; reduce heat. Cook, uncovered, for 7 minutes. Add asparagus to broth; cook 3 minutes more. Meanwhile, remove chicken from bones. Discard skin and bones. Shred chicken into bite-size pieces.

3 Stir cooked chicken, Swiss chard, tomatoes, and ham into Dutch oven. Heat through. Season to taste with salt and pepper. Sprinkle with chives and parsley.

Nutrition Facts per serving: 286 calories, 8 g total fat, 44 mg cholesterol, 1,115 mg sodium, 26 g carbohydrate, 25 g protein.

Tex-Mex Tortilla Soup

This recipe makes six main-dish portions for a light luncheon entrée. You can also serve smaller portions as an appetizer for your next Mexican-themed dinner party.

Prep: 25 minutes

Cook: 20 minutes

Makes: 6 servings

2 14½-ounce cans reduced-sodium chicken broth

1 14½-ounce can beef broth

1 14½-ounce can tomatoes, undrained and cut up

1 medium onion, chopped (½ cup)

¼ cup chopped green sweet pepper

4 medium skinless, boneless chicken breast halves (about 1 pound total), cut into bite-size pieces

1 cup frozen loose-pack whole kernel corn

1 to 2 teaspoons chili powder

½ teaspoon ground cumin

⅛ teaspoon ground black pepper

3 cups tortilla chips, coarsely crushed

1 cup shredded Monterey Jack cheese (4 ounces)

1 avocado, peeled, seeded, and cut into chunks (optional)

Snipped fresh cilantro (optional)

Sliced fresh jalapeño chile peppers (optional) (see tip, page 176)

Lime wedges (optional)

1 In a 4-quart Dutch oven combine chicken broth, beef broth, undrained tomatoes, onion, and sweet pepper. Bring to boiling. Add chicken. Return to boiling; reduce heat. Simmer, covered, for 10 minutes. Add corn, chili powder, cumin, and black pepper. Return to boiling; reduce heat. Simmer, covered, for 10 minutes more.

2 To serve, divide crushed tortilla chips among six soup bowls. Ladle soup over tortilla chips. Sprinkle with cheese. If desired, top with avocado, cilantro, and sliced jalapeño peppers, and serve with lime wedges.

Nutrition Facts per serving: 259 calories, 10 g total fat, 60 mg cholesterol, 896 mg sodium, 17 g carbohydrate, 27 g protein.

Catalan Chicken Chowder

Time-pressed cooks will appreciate the way this colorful soup starts with a pre-seasoned yellow rice mix. For dessert, serve flan (also known as crème caramel), and you'll enjoy a classic Catalan-style dinner.

Start to Finish: 45 minutes

Makes: 4 servings

- 1 5-ounce package saffron-flavored yellow rice mix
- 8 ounces skinless, boneless chicken breast halves, cut into bite-size pieces
- ½ cup chopped onion
- 1 clove garlic, minced
- 2 teaspoons olive oil
- 1 14½-ounce can diced tomatoes
- 1 14½-ounce can reduced-sodium chicken broth
- ½ of a 14-ounce can artichoke hearts, drained and quartered (about ¾ cup)
- ½ cup loose-pack frozen baby sweet peas
- ½ of a 7-ounce jar roasted red sweet peppers, drained and cut into strips
- 2 tablespoons slivered almonds, toasted (see tip, page 226)

1 Prepare rice mix according to package directions; set aside and keep warm. Meanwhile, in a large saucepan cook chicken, onion, and garlic in hot oil over medium-high heat about 5 minutes or until chicken is no longer pink.

2 Add undrained tomatoes, broth, and artichoke hearts to chicken mixture. Bring to boiling; reduce heat. Simmer, uncovered, for 10 minutes, stirring occasionally. Add peas and peppers. Cook for 3 to 4 minutes more or until heated through.

3 To serve, ladle chowder into bowls. Spoon a mound of cooked rice into the center of each serving. Sprinkle with almonds.

Nutrition Facts per serving: 321 calories, 10 g total fat, 30 mg cholesterol, 1,099 mg sodium, 42 g carbohydrate, 19 g protein.

Moroccan Bouillabaisse

Hints of cinnamon and cumin mingle with seafood and couscous, giving this version of a South-of-France stew some North African flourishes.

Prep: 30 minutes

Stand: 45 minutes

Cook: 5 minutes

Makes: 4 servings

8 ounces fresh or frozen shrimp with tails, peeled and deveined

8 ounces fresh or frozen scallops

8 ounces (8 to 12) fresh mussels in shells

1 cup finely chopped onion

4 cloves garlic, minced

1 tablespoon olive oil

1 teaspoon ground cumin

½ teaspoon ground cinnamon

¼ teaspoon ground red pepper

1 cup fish or vegetable broth

1 cup finely chopped tomatoes

⅛ teaspoon ground saffron

¼ teaspoon salt

Hot cooked couscous

Fresh parsley sprigs (optional)

1 Thaw frozen seafood. Halve large scallops. Scrub mussels; remove beards. Combine 2 cups water and 3 tablespoons salt; soak mussels 15 minutes. Drain; rinse. Repeat twice.

2 Cook onion and garlic in hot oil until tender. Add cumin, cinnamon, and red pepper; cook and stir 1 minute. Stir in broth, tomatoes, saffron, and ¼ teaspoon salt. Bring to boiling; add seafood. Return to boiling; reduce heat. Simmer, covered, 5 minutes or until mussel shells open and shrimp and scallops are opaque. Discard any mussels with unopened shells. Serve with couscous. If desired, top with parsley sprigs.

Nutrition Facts per serving: 187 calories, 6 g total fat, 116 mg cholesterol, 503 mg sodium, 12 g carbohydrate, 23 g protein.

Shrimp Tortilla Soup

Here, the popular tortilla soup garners extra praise with some sweet shrimp in the mix.

Start to Finish: 50 minutes

Makes: 4 servings

5 6-inch corn tortillas

Cooking oil

2 medium carrots, cut into thin strips (1 cup)

4 green onions, sliced

3 cloves garlic, minced

2 14½-ounce cans reduced-sodium chicken broth

1 14½-ounce can diced tomatoes

¼ cup snipped cilantro

¼ teaspoon ground black pepper

8 ounces fresh or frozen shrimp in shells, thawed, peeled, and deveined

1 cup shredded Monterey Jack cheese or crumbled queso fresco (4 ounces) (optional)

Chopped avocado (optional)

Fresh cilantro sprigs (optional)

1 Cut tortillas into ½-inch strips. (Use craft scissors to create a decorative edge, if desired.) In a large skillet pour cooking oil to a depth of ¼ inch; heat over medium-high heat. Fry tortilla strips, a few at a time, in hot oil about 1½ minutes or until brown and crisp. Transfer the strips with a slotted spoon to paper towels; drain thoroughly.* Set aside.

2 In a large Dutch oven cook carrots, onions, and garlic in 1 tablespoon hot oil about 5 minutes, stirring frequently. Stir in chicken broth, undrained diced tomatoes, snipped cilantro, and pepper. Bring to boiling; reduce heat and simmer, covered, 10 minutes.

3 Meanwhile, place half of the tortilla strips in a food processor bowl or blender container; cover and process or blend until tortilla strips are finely crushed. Stir crushed tortillas into the soup; cover and cook 5 minutes more.

4 Stir in shrimp; cook 1 to 3 minutes or until shrimp are opaque. If desired, stir in Monterey Jack cheese or queso fresco until melted.

5 To serve, ladle into soup bowls. Top the soup with the remaining tortilla strips and, if desired, garnish with avocado and cilantro sprigs.

*Note: If you prefer not to fry the tortilla strips, place the strips on an ungreased baking sheet. Bake in a 350°F oven for 15 minutes or until crisp, stirring once.

Nutrition Facts per serving: 254 calories, 13 g total fat, 65 mg cholesterol, 967 mg sodium, 25 g carbohydrate, 12 g protein.

Creamy Clam-Scallop Chowder

Here, elegance and heartiness combine in one lovely soup! A Caesar salad and some flavorful rye dinner rolls would make winning accompaniments.

Start to Finish: 45 minutes

Makes: 4 servings

- 6 ounces fresh or frozen bay scallops
- 1 pint shucked clams or two 6½-ounce cans minced clams
- 3 slices bacon, halved crosswise
- 2½ cups chopped, peeled potatoes
- 1 cup chopped shallots or finely chopped onion
- 1 tablespoon snipped fresh dill or 1 teaspoon dried dill
- 1 teaspoon instant chicken bouillon granules
- ⅛ teaspoon ground black pepper
- 2 cups milk
- 1 cup half-and-half or light cream
- 2 tablespoons all-purpose flour
- ¼ cup shredded carrot
- 2 tablespoons dry sherry
- Fresh dill sprigs (optional)

1 Thaw scallops, if frozen. Chop shucked clams (if using), reserving juice; set clams aside. Strain clam juice to remove bits of shell. (Or, drain canned clams, reserving juice.) If necessary, add water to clam juice to equal 1 cup. Set clam juice mixture aside.

2 In a large saucepan or Dutch oven cook bacon until crisp. Remove bacon, reserving 1 tablespoon drippings, if desired. Drain bacon on paper towels; crumble. Set bacon aside.

3 In the same saucepan combine reserved bacon drippings (if desired), reserved clam juice mixture, potatoes, shallots or onion, dill, bouillon granules, and pepper. Bring to boiling; reduce heat. Simmer, covered, about 10 minutes or until potatoes are tender. With the back of a fork, mash potatoes slightly against the side of the pan.

4 Combine milk, half-and-half or light cream, and flour until smooth. Add to potato mixture along with shredded carrot. Cook and stir until slightly thickened and bubbly. Stir in clams and scallops. Return to boiling. Reduce heat; cook, uncovered, for 1 to 2 minutes more or until clams curl around the edges and scallops are opaque. Stir in sherry.

5 To serve, ladle soup into bowls. Sprinkle each serving with crumbled bacon and, if desired, garnish with additional dill.

Nutrition Facts per serving: 420 calories, 13 g total fat, 86 mg cholesterol, 518 mg sodium, 43 g carbohydrate, 31 g protein.

Sicilian Seafood Stew

Basil, oregano, and marjoram are favorite herbs of Mediterranean cooks. Combined with garlic, the herb trio adds a windfall of flavor to this robust stew.

Prep: 20 minutes

Cook: 18 minutes

Makes: 4 to 6 servings

1 cup chopped onion

1 cup chopped celery

¾ cup chopped green sweet pepper

¾ cup chopped red sweet pepper

2 tablespoons olive oil or cooking oil

3 cloves garlic, minced

1 teaspoon dried basil, crushed

½ teaspoon dried oregano, crushed

½ teaspoon dried marjoram, crushed

⅛ teaspoon crushed red pepper or dash ground red pepper

1 28-ounce can tomatoes, cut up

1 8-ounce bottle clam juice

⅓ cup dry red wine

½ pound fresh scallops, rinsed

½ pound fresh peeled and deveined shrimp

2 tablespoons lemon juice

Lemon slices (optional)

Fresh oregano sprigs (optional)

1 In a Dutch oven, cook onion, celery, and sweet peppers in olive oil over high heat about 5 minutes or until tender, stirring constantly. Stir in garlic, basil, oregano, marjoram, and crushed red pepper or ground red pepper. Reduce heat, cover, and cook for 2 minutes. Add undrained tomatoes, clam juice, and wine. Simmer, covered, for 15 minutes.

2 Cut up any large scallops. Add scallops and shrimp to Dutch oven; cover and cook about 3 minutes or until the scallops and shrimp are opaque. Stir in the lemon juice.

3 To serve, ladle into bowls. If desired, garnish with lemon slices and fresh oregano.

Nutrition Facts per serving: 239 calories, 8 g total fat, 104 mg cholesterol, 687 mg sodium, 20 g carbohydrate, 20 g protein.

Salmon Pan Chowder

You'll want to seek out wide, shallow bowls for this striking yet simple way to serve salmon.

Prep: 25 minutes

Cook: 35 minutes

Makes: 4 servings

Nonstick cooking spray

1¼ cups white and/or purple pearl onions, peeled

1 medium red sweet pepper, cut into ½-inch strips* (1 cup)

1 medium yellow sweet pepper, cut into ½-inch strips (1 cup)

1 medium green sweet pepper, cut into ½-inch strips* (1 cup)

1 large banana pepper, cut into ¼-inch rings (see tip, page 176)

1 14½-ounce can vegetable broth or chicken broth

1 cup whipping cream

½ teaspoon caraway seeds, lightly crushed

¼ teaspoon salt

4 2-ounce skinless, boneless salmon fillets

Fresh dill sprigs

1 Coat an unheated Dutch oven with nonstick cooking spray; heat pan. Add onions. Cook and stir, uncovered, over medium-high heat about 7 minutes or until tender. Add red pepper, yellow pepper, green pepper, and banana pepper. Cook and stir for 1 minute more. Carefully add broth. Bring just to boiling; reduce heat. Simmer, uncovered, for 10 minutes. Stir in whipping cream. Return to boiling; reduce heat. Simmer for 10 minutes.

2 Meanwhile, rub caraway seeds and salt on both sides of fish. Coat an unheated skillet with nonstick cooking spray; heat skillet. Cook fillets, uncovered, over medium-high heat for 3 to 4 minutes per side or until fish flakes easily when tested with a fork. Remove. Cover; keep warm.

3 To serve, place a salmon fillet in each of four shallow soup bowls. Ladle soup mixture over salmon fillets. Top with dill sprigs.

*****Note:** For extra pepper pep, substitute a dark green poblano chile pepper and a red jalapeño chile pepper for the green sweet pepper and red sweet pepper. For tips on handling hot peppers, see page 176.

Nutrition Facts per serving: 327 calories, 25 g total fat, 112 mg cholesterol, 647 mg sodium, 14 g carbohydrate, 15 g protein.

Crab Chowder

The ultimate catch of the day—crab—stars in a better-than-ever version of chowder that's made extra rich with cream cheese and extra flavorful with bouquet garni seasoning.

Start to Finish: 25 minutes

Makes: 4 servings

1 6-ounce package frozen crabmeat or one 6-ounce can crabmeat, drained, flaked, and cartilage removed

1 medium zucchini, cut into 2-inch strips

1 medium red or green sweet pepper, chopped (¾ cup)

2 tablespoons margarine or butter

2 tablespoons all-purpose flour

4 cups milk

2 tablespoons sliced green onion

½ teaspoon bouquet garni seasoning

¼ teaspoon salt

⅛ teaspoon ground black pepper

1 3-ounce package cream cheese, cut up

1 teaspoon snipped fresh thyme

Fresh thyme sprigs (optional)

1 Thaw crabmeat, if frozen. In a medium saucepan cook zucchini and sweet pepper in hot margarine until crisp-tender. Stir in the flour. Add the milk, green onion, bouquet garni seasoning, salt, and black pepper.

2 Cook and stir over medium-high heat until thickened and bubbly. Add the cream cheese; cook and stir until cream cheese melts. Stir in the crabmeat and snipped thyme; heat through.

3 To serve, ladle into soup bowls. If desired, garnish each serving with fresh thyme sprigs.

Nutrition Facts per serving: 314 calories, 19 g total fat, 64 mg cholesterol, 844 mg sodium, 18 g carbohydrate, 19 g protein.

Mushroom Tortelloni in Curry Cream

Serve this quick soup, flavored with Indonesian touches of curry, coconut, and basil, for an informal Sunday night soup party with friends.

Start to Finish: 30 minutes

Makes: 4 servings

1 shallot, finely chopped

1 fresh jalapeño chile pepper, seeded and finely chopped (see tip, page 176)

2 teaspoons curry powder

1 clove garlic, minced

1 tablespoon cooking oil

1 14½-ounce can chicken broth

1 13½- or 14-ounce can unsweetened coconut milk

1 9-ounce package refrigerated mushroom-filled tortelloni*

1 tablespoon snipped fresh basil

1 medium tomato, chopped (½ cup)

Chopped peanuts (optional)

1 In a medium saucepan cook shallot, jalapeño pepper, curry powder, and garlic in hot oil about 1 minute or until shallot is tender. Stir in chicken broth. Bring to boiling; reduce heat. Simmer, covered, for 5 minutes.

2 Stir in the coconut milk, tortelloni, and basil. Cook and stir about 5 minutes more or until pasta is tender but still firm. Stir in the tomato. Cook and stir until heated through, but do not boil.

3 To serve, ladle into bowls. If desired, sprinkle with chopped peanuts.

*Note: If you're unable to find tortelloni, a larger version of tortellini, use tortellini instead.

Nutrition Facts per serving: 306 calories, 14 g total fat, 24 mg cholesterol, 649 mg sodium, 35 g carbohydrate, 10 g protein.

Cream of Asparagus Soup, **recipe page 228**

Turn here for refreshing soups that showcase the colorful bounty of summer gardens.

Summer-Fresh Soups

Dilled Spinach Soup

A little meat elevates this cold soup to main-dish status. Serve with croissants and fresh fruit for dessert, and you'll have a relaxing, heat-beating supper for the dog days of summer.

Start to Finish: 20 minutes

Makes: 4 main-dish servings

9 **cups packaged prewashed spinach (about 10 ounces)**

2 **cups milk**

1 **small onion, cut up**

2 **tablespoons snipped fresh dill**

1 **teaspoon lemon-pepper seasoning**

2 **8-ounce cartons plain fat-free yogurt**

1 **cup cubed cooked turkey or ham, or cooked small shrimp**

Edible flowers (such as nasturtiums) and/or slivered almonds, toasted (see tip, at right) (optional)

1 In a blender container or food processor bowl combine about one-third of the spinach, 1 cup of the milk, the onion, dill, and lemon-pepper seasoning. Cover and blend or process until nearly smooth. Add another one-third of the spinach; cover and blend until smooth. Pour blended mixture into a serving bowl or large storage container.

2 In the blender container or food processor bowl combine the remaining spinach, remaining milk, and the yogurt. Cover and blend until nearly smooth. Stir into the mixture in serving bowl; stir in the turkey. Serve immediately or cover and store in the refrigerator up to 24 hours.

3 To serve, ladle into soup bowls. If desired, garnish each serving with edible flowers and/or toasted almonds.

Nutrition Facts per serving: 217 calories, 6 g total fat, 45 mg cholesterol, 508 mg sodium, 18 g carbohydrate, 24 g protein.

TOASTING NUTS AND SEEDS

Toasting heightens the flavors of nuts and seeds. To toast, spread the food in a single layer in a shallow baking pan. Bake in a 350°F oven for 5 to 10 minutes or until light golden brown, watching carefully and stirring once or twice.

Cream of Asparagus Soup

Often creamed vegetable soups taste more like cream or butter than vegetables. Not this one! With an entire pound of asparagus, the sprightly flavor of the spears really comes through.

Prep: 25 minutes

Cook: 25 minutes

Makes: 6 side-dish servings

3 cups water

1 tablespoon instant chicken bouillon granules

2 large stalks fresh lemongrass, cut into 2-inch pieces, or 2 teaspoons finely shredded lemon peel

2 tablespoons snipped fresh cilantro

¼ teaspoon ground white pepper

1 pound fresh asparagus, trimmed and cut into 2-inch pieces

1 12-ounce can (1½ cups) evaporated fat-free milk

2 tablespoons cornstarch

Dairy sour cream (optional)

1 In a medium saucepan stir together the water, bouillon granules, fresh lemongrass or lemon peel, fresh cilantro, and white pepper. Bring to boiling; reduce heat to low. Simmer, covered, for 15 minutes. Strain the liquid, discarding the solids; return the liquid to the saucepan.

2 Return liquid to boiling. Set aside a few of the asparagus tips for garnish. Add the remaining asparagus to saucepan. Reduce heat to low. Simmer, uncovered, for 8 to 10 minutes or until asparagus is tender. Remove from heat; cool slightly.

3 Carefully transfer the asparagus-broth mixture to a blender container.* Cover and blend until smooth; set aside.

4 In the same saucepan gradually stir the evaporated milk into the cornstarch. Cook and stir over medium heat until thickened and bubbly. Cook and stir for 2 minutes more. (The mixture may be slightly foamy.) Gradually add the asparagus mixture, stirring constantly. Heat through.

5 To serve, ladle into soup bowls. If desired, swirl a little dairy sour cream into each serving and top with the reserved asparagus tips.

*Note: For information on blending and pureeing soups, see page 5.

Nutrition Facts per serving: 131 calories, 4 g total fat, 3 mg cholesterol, 581 mg sodium, 15 g carbohydrate, 8 g protein.

Snap Pea and Asparagus Pasta Soup

This light and luscious soup is a great way to use sugar-snap peas and asparagus—two of spring and early summer's best garden treasures.

Start to Finish: 30 minutes

Makes: 4 main-dish servings

4 cups reduced-sodium chicken broth

2 cups water

2 slightly beaten eggs

2 teaspoons cooking oil

4 ounces dried angel hair pasta, broken into 2-inch pieces

2 medium leeks, sliced, or ⅔ cup sliced green onions

2 cloves garlic, minced

4 ounces sugar snap peas, strings and tips removed and halved crosswise

8 ounces asparagus, trimmed and cut into 1-inch pieces (about 1 cup)

2 tablespoons snipped fresh dill

2 teaspoons finely shredded lemon peel

Medium asparagus spears, trimmed (optional)

1 In a large saucepan bring the chicken broth and the water to boiling.

2 Meanwhile, in a medium skillet cook eggs in hot oil over medium heat, without stirring, for 2 to 3 minutes or until eggs are set. To remove cooked eggs, loosen edge and invert skillet over a cutting board; cut eggs into thin, bite-size strips. Set aside.

3 Add pasta, leeks, and garlic to chicken broth. Boil gently, uncovered, about 3 minutes or until pasta is almost tender. Add sugar snap peas, asparagus pieces, dill, and lemon peel. Return to boiling. Boil gently about 2 minutes or until vegetables are crisp-tender. Stir in egg strips.

4 To serve, ladle into soup bowls. If desired, garnish with trimmed asparagus spears.

Nutrition Facts per serving: 235 calories, 7 g total fat, 107 mg cholesterol, 684 mg sodium, 33 g carbohydrate, 12 g protein.

Crab and Pasta Gazpacho

Gazpacho traditionally hails from Spain, but cooks in this country have recreated it in a variety of versions. This one, with nectarines, basil, and sweet crabmeat, is one of the most clever American takes.

Start to Finish: 25 minutes

Makes: 6 main-dish servings

1 cup dried small shell macaroni or bow-tie pasta (4 ounces)

4 cups hot-style vegetable juice, chilled

1 tablespoon lime juice or lemon juice

6 ounces cooked lump crabmeat, flaked, or chopped cooked chicken (about 1¼ cups)

2 medium nectarines, chopped (1⅓ cups)

2 plum tomatoes, chopped

¼ cup chopped, seeded cucumber

2 tablespoons snipped fresh basil

Lime wedges (optional)

1 Cook pasta according to package directions; drain in colander. Rinse with cold water; drain again.

2 Meanwhile, in a large bowl stir together vegetable juice and lime juice. Stir in pasta, crabmeat, nectarines, tomatoes, cucumber, and basil.

3 To serve, ladle into soup bowls. If desired, serve with lime wedges.

Nutrition Facts per serving: 162 calories, 1 g total fat, 28 mg cholesterol, 947 mg sodium, 28 g carbohydrate, 11 g protein.

Gazpacho

Chickpeas add an extra heartiness to this version of the all-time favorite summer soup.

Prep: 30 minutes

Chill: 2 hours

Makes: 6 side-dish servings

1 15-ounce can chunky Italian- or salsa-style tomatoes

2 cups quartered yellow pear-shape and/or halved cherry tomatoes

1 15-ounce can chickpeas (garbanzo beans), rinsed and drained

1¼ cups hot-style vegetable juice or vegetable juice

1 cup beef broth

½ cup coarsely chopped, seeded cucumber

½ cup coarsely chopped yellow and/or red sweet pepper

¼ cup coarsely chopped red onion

¼ cup snipped fresh cilantro

3 tablespoons lime juice or lemon juice

2 cloves garlic, minced

¼ to ½ teaspoon bottled hot pepper sauce

1 In a large bowl combine canned and fresh tomatoes, chickpeas, vegetable juice, broth, cucumber, sweet pepper, onion, cilantro, lime or lemon juice, garlic, and hot pepper sauce. Cover and chill for at least 2 hours or up to 24 hours.

2 To serve, ladle soup into bowls or mugs.

Nutrition Facts per serving : 142 calories, 5 g total fat, 0 mg cholesterol, 1,145 mg sodium, 27 g carbohydrate, 7 g protein.

Cucumber Yogurt-Mint Soup

Serve this no-cook soup alongside a Greek salad for a refreshing summer supper.

Prep: 15 minutes

Chill: 2 hours

Makes: 4 side-dish servings

1 large cucumber

1 8-ounce carton plain low-fat yogurt

1 tablespoon lime juice

1 teaspoon honey

½ teaspoon ground cumin

¼ teaspoon salt

2 tablespoons milk (optional)

⅓ cup snipped fresh mint

Fresh mint sprigs

1 Peel the cucumber, then cut in half lengthwise. Scoop out seeds and discard. Cut cucumber into ½-inch slices (1½ cups). In a blender container or food processor bowl combine cucumber, yogurt, lime juice, honey, cumin, and salt. Cover and blend or process until smooth. If desired, blend in milk. Stir in snipped mint. Cover and chill for at least 2 hours or up to 24 hours.

2 To serve, stir before serving. Ladle into soup bowls. Garnish with fresh mint sprigs.

Nutrition Facts per serving: 56 calories, 1 g total fat, 3 mg cholesterol, 176 mg sodium, 8 g carbohydrate, 4 g protein.

Creamy Carrot Soup with Pesto

What did American cooks ever do without pesto? Fresh-tasting and easy to use, it's the ultimate convenience product. You'll love the burst of flavor it brings to this soup.

Start to Finish: 45 minutes

Makes: 4 side-dish servings

½ cup chopped onion

1 tablespoon margarine or butter

1 cup sliced carrots

¼ teaspoon dried thyme, crushed

1 clove garlic, crushed

3 cups chicken broth

1 cup cubed, peeled potatoes

1 small bay leaf

2 tablespoons buttermilk

2 tablespoons pesto

1 In a large saucepan cook the onion in hot margarine 1 minute. Add carrots, thyme, and garlic; cook 10 minutes or until tender. Carefully add broth, potatoes, and bay leaf. Bring to boiling; reduce heat. Simmer, covered, about 20 minutes or until vegetables are tender. Discard the bay leaf.

2 Transfer about half of the mixture to a blender container or food processor bowl.* Cover and blend or process until smooth. Repeat with remaining soup. Return all soup to sauce pan; add buttermilk and heat through.

3 To serve, ladle into soup bowls. Top each serving with pesto; swirl to mix.

*Note: For information on blending and pureeing soups, see page 5.

Nutrition Facts per serving: 134 calories, 6 g total fat, 10 mg cholesterol, 655 mg sodium, 15 g carbohydrate, 6 g protein.

Carrot and Chile Pepper Soup

Green chile peppers, chili powder, and cumin give this creamy carrot soup a special spark.

Start to Finish: 30 minutes

Makes: 8 side-dish servings

2   14½-ounce cans vegetable broth

16   ounces packaged peeled baby
carrots

1   large onion, chopped (1 cup)

1   4-ounce can diced green chile
peppers

1   teaspoon chili powder

½   teaspoon ground cumin

1   cup half-and-half or light cream
Fresh purple basil leaves
(optional)

1 In a large saucepan or Dutch oven combine broth, carrots, onion, chile peppers, chili powder, and cumin. Bring mixture to boiling; reduce heat. Simmer, covered, 12 minutes or until carrots are very tender. Cool mixture slightly.

2 Transfer about half of the mixture to a blender container or food processor bowl.* Cover and blend or process until smooth. Repeat with remaining soup. Return mixture to saucepan. Stir in half-and-half or light cream. Heat through.

3 To serve, ladle soup into bowls. If desired, garnish with purple basil.

*Note: For information on blending and pureeing soups, see page 5.

Nutrition Facts per serving: 75 calories, 4 g total fat, 11 mg cholesterol, 510 mg sodium, 10 g carbohydrate, 2 g protein.

Two-Tomato Soup

This recipe makes two batches—one to enjoy as soon as fresh homegrown tomatoes are in season, the other to savor later in the year, when summer's bumper crop is but a memory.

Prep: 45 minutes

Cook: 1 hour 5 minutes

Makes: 8 side-dish servings total (2 batches of 4 portions)

1 3-ounce package dried tomatoes (not oil-packed)

½ cup chopped onion

¼ teaspoon coarsely ground black pepper

1 tablespoon olive oil or cooking oil

8 medium fresh tomatoes, chopped (about 2½ pounds)

4 cups water

1 teaspoon salt

½ cup whipping cream

Olive oil (optional)

8 yellow teardrop or dried yellow tomato halves (optional)

1 Place the dried tomatoes in a small bowl. Add enough boiling water to cover. Soak them for 30 minutes. Drain and rinse. Coarsely chop rehydrated tomatoes.

2 In a Dutch oven cook and stir onion, rehydrated tomatoes, and pepper in 1 tablespoon olive oil or cooking oil about 5 minutes or until onion is tender. Reserve ¾ cup chopped fresh tomatoes; set aside. Add remaining fresh tomatoes to rehydrated tomato mixture. Cook, covered, over low heat about 20 minutes or until tomatoes are soft. Add the water and salt. Cook, uncovered, over low heat for 40 minutes more, stirring often.

3 Transfer one-fourth of mixture at a time to a blender container or food processor bowl.* Cover and carefully blend or process until smooth. Return mixture to Dutch oven. Heat to simmering.

4 Remove half of the soup mixture; cool slightly. Transfer to freezer containers. Seal, label, and freeze up to 2 months.**

5 To serve remaining soup, stir cream into soup. Heat just until simmering. Ladle soup into bowls. Spoon some of the reserved fresh chopped tomatoes into each bowl. If desired, drizzle each serving with some olive oil and top with a yellow teardrop tomato half.

***Note:** For information on blending and pureeing soups, see page 5.

****Note:** To reheat frozen portion, transfer to a saucepan. Cook, covered, over medium heat for 15 to 20 minutes, stirring occasionally. Stir in ½ cup cream. Cook and stir 5 to 10 minutes more or until heated through. To serve, ladle into soup bowls as directed.

Nutrition Facts per serving: 176 calories, 14 g total fat, 41 mg cholesterol, 540 mg sodium, 13 g carbohydrate, 3 g protein.

Tomato-Basil Soup

Italian cooks love to pair tomatoes and basil—and this unbelievably fresh-tasting recipe follows that delicious lead! If you have a hard time finding fresh basil, experiment with other herbs that are flourishing in your garden or at the market.

Start to Finish: 40 minutes

Makes: 4 main-dish servings

2 medium carrots, finely chopped (1 cup)

2 stalks celery, finely chopped (1 cup)

1 large onion, finely chopped (1 cup)

6 cloves garlic, minced

1 tablespoon olive oil

1 cup water

2 pounds tomatoes, chopped (about 6 cups)

½ cup snipped fresh basil or 2 tablespoons dried basil, crushed, and ½ cup snipped fresh parsley

1 teaspoon salt

1 tablespoon balsamic vinegar

1 In a covered large saucepan cook carrots, celery, onion, and garlic in hot oil over medium-low heat for 10 minutes, stirring occasionally. Transfer to a blender container or food processor bowl;* add the water. Cover and blend or process until smooth. Return to saucepan.

2 Stir in half of the tomatoes, half of the fresh basil or all of the dried basil, and the salt. Bring to boiling; reduce heat. Simmer, covered, for 15 minutes. Remove from heat.

3 Stir in the remaining tomatoes, the remaining fresh basil or all of the parsley, and the balsamic vinegar; heat through.

*Note: For information on blending and pureeing soups, see page 5.

Nutrition Facts per serving: 145 calories, 5 g total fat, 0 mg cholesterol, 618 mg sodium, 26 g carbohydrate, 4 g protein.

Yellow Pepper Soup with Yogurt and Cucumbers

Fennel seeds and cardamom add a note of sophistication to garden-ripe yellow sweet peppers.

Start to Finish: 40 minutes

Makes: 4 side-dish servings

1 8-ounce carton plain or low-fat yogurt (do not use nonfat)

1 teaspoon fennel seeds, crushed

4 to 7 medium yellow sweet peppers, seeded and coarsely chopped (about 5 cups)

¼ cup chopped shallots

¾ teaspoon ground cardamom

2 tablespoons olive oil

1 14-ounce can reduced-sodium chicken broth

1 cup water

2 tablespoons cider vinegar

¼ cup coarsely chopped cucumber

Fennel seeds

1 In a small bowl stir together the yogurt and the 1 teaspoon fennel seeds. Cover and let stand at room temperature for 30 minutes.

2 Meanwhile, in a large saucepan cook the yellow peppers, shallots, and cardamom in the hot oil about 15 minutes or just until peppers are beginning to soften, stirring occasionally. Add broth, the water, and vinegar. Bring to boiling; reduce heat. Simmer, covered, for 5 minutes more. Remove from heat and allow to cool slightly.

3 Transfer half of the pepper mixture to a blender container or food processor bowl.* Cover and blend or process until smooth. Repeat with remaining pepper mixture. Return all to saucepan.** Cook and stir over medium heat until heated through.

4 To serve, ladle soup into bowls. Top with yogurt mixture, cucumber, and additional fennel seeds.

*Note: For information on blending and pureeing soups, see page 5.

**Note: If desired, transfer soup to a bowl. Cover and chill in the refrigerator for at least 1 hour or up to 24 hours.

Nutrition Facts per serving: 154 calories, 9 g total fat, 8 mg cholesterol, 306 mg sodium, 15 g carbohydrate, 5 g protein.

Sweet-Potato Pear Vichyssoise

Serve this delicate pear-and-potato soup cold as you would traditional vichyssoise for summer meals, or warmed to start off a winter menu.

Start to Finish: 40 minutes

Makes: 6 side-dish servings

- 2 medium leeks, sliced (⅔ cup)
- 1 tablespoon margarine or butter
- 2 medium sweet potatoes, peeled and cubed (2 cups)
- 1 14-ounce can chicken broth
- 1 medium pear, peeled and chopped (¾ cup)
- 1 teaspoon snipped fresh thyme or ¼ teaspoon dried thyme, crushed
- ⅛ teaspoon salt
- ⅛ teaspoon ground black pepper
- 1 cup half-and-half or light cream
  Pear slices (optional)
  Fresh thyme sprigs (optional)

1 In a saucepan cook and stir leeks in margarine or butter over medium heat until tender. Stir in sweet potatoes, broth, the chopped pear, the snipped or dried thyme, salt, and black pepper. Bring to boiling; reduce heat. Simmer, covered, for 25 to 35 minutes or until potatoes are very tender. Remove from heat and cool slightly.

2 Transfer half the sweet potato mixture in a blender container or food processor bowl.* Cover and blend or process until smooth. Repeat with remaining mixture. Stir half-and-half or light cream into the sweet-potato mixture. Place sweet potato mixture in a covered container.** Chill in the refrigerator for at least 4 hours or up to 24 hours.

3 To serve, if desired, garnish with pear slices and a thyme sprig.

*Note:: For information on blending and pureeing soups, see page 5.

**Note: To serve the soup warm, return sweet potato mixture to saucepan. Heat through.

Nutrition Facts per serving: 151 calories, 7 g total fat, 15 mg cholesterol, 309 mg sodium, 19 g carbohydrate, 4 g protein.

Chilly Fruit Soup

Rhubarb and cantaloupe make this blissful bowl pretty and sweet, while a little black pepper and fresh ginger lend a spicy contrast to this succulent summer soup.

Prep: 20 minutes
Chill: 3 hours
Makes: 6 side-dish servings

½ **cup sugar**

¼ **cup water**

1 **tablespoon grated fresh ginger**

⅛ **teaspoon ground black pepper**

2 **cups fresh or frozen rhubarb, cut into ½-inch slices**

1 **medium cantaloupe, peeled, seeded, and cut up (about 4 cups)**

¾ **cup orange juice**

1 **8-ounce carton plain low-fat yogurt**

Fresh mint sprigs (optional)

1 In a medium saucepan combine sugar, the water, fresh ginger, and pepper; bring to boiling. Add rhubarb. Return to boiling; reduce heat. Simmer, covered, about 5 minutes or until rhubarb is tender. (Do not drain.) Remove from heat; let cool.

2 In a blender container or food processor bowl,* place about half of the cantaloupe and half of the orange juice. Cover and blend or process until smooth. Add about half of the cooled rhubarb mixture and half of the yogurt. Cover and process until smooth. Transfer to a large bowl. Repeat with remaining portions.

3 Cover and chill soup in the refrigerator for several hours or until cold. To serve, ladle soup into bowls. If desired, garnish with fresh mint.

*****Note:** If using a food processor, you may need to process one-third at a time, especially if the bowl has a smaller capacity. For information on blending and pureeing soups, see page 5.

Nutrition Facts per serving: 149 calories, 1 g total fat, 2 mg cholesterol, 39 mg sodium, 34 g carbohydrate, 4 g protein.

Index

Metric Information

The charts on this page provide a guide for converting measurements from the U.S. customary system, which is used throughout this book, to the metric system.

Product Differences

Most of the ingredients called for in the recipes in this book are available in most countries. However, some are known by different names. Here are some common American ingredients and their possible counterparts:

- Sugar (white) is granulated, fine granulated, or castor sugar.
- Powdered sugar is icing sugar.
- All-purpose flour is enriched, bleached or unbleached white household flour. When self-rising flour is used in place of all-purpose flour in a recipe that calls for leavening, omit the leavening agent (baking soda or baking powder) and salt.
- Light-colored corn syrup is golden syrup.
- Cornstarch is cornflour.
- Baking soda is bicarbonate of soda.
- Vanilla or vanilla extract is vanilla essence.
- Green, red, or yellow sweet peppers are capsicums or bell peppers.
- Golden raisins are sultanas.

Volume and Weight

The United States traditionally uses cup measures for liquid and solid ingredients. The chart below shows the approximate imperial and metric equivalents. If you are accustomed to weighing solid ingredients, the following approximate equivalents will be helpful.

- 1 cup butter, castor sugar, or rice = 8 ounces = ½ pound = 250 grams
- 1 cup flour = 4 ounces = ¼ pound = 125 grams
- 1 cup icing sugar = 5 ounces = 150 grams

Canadian and U.S. volume for a cup measure is 8 fluid ounces (237 ml), but the standard metric equivalent is 250 ml.

1 British imperial cup is 10 fluid ounces.

In Australia, 1 tablespoon equals 20 ml, and there are 4 teaspoons in the Australian tablespoon.

Spoon measures are used for smaller amounts of ingredients. Although the size of the tablespoon varies slightly in different countries, for practical purposes and for recipes in this book, a straight substitution is all that's necessary. Measurements made using cups or spoons always should be level unless stated otherwise.

Common Weight Range Replacements

Imperial / U.S.	Metric
½ ounce	15 g
1 ounce	25 g or 30 g
4 ounces (¼ pound)	115 g or 125 g
8 ounces (½ pound)	225 g or 250 g
16 ounces (1 pound)	450 g or 500 g
1¼ pounds	625 g
1½ pounds	750 g
2 pounds or 2¼ pounds	1,000 g or 1 Kg

Oven Temperature Equivalents

Fahrenheit Setting	Celsius Setting*	Gas Setting
300°F	150°C	Gas Mark 2 (very low)
325°F	160°C	Gas Mark 3 (low)
350°F	180°C	Gas Mark 4 (moderate)
375°F	190°C	Gas Mark 5 (moderate)
400°F	200°C	Gas Mark 6 (hot)
425°F	220°C	Gas Mark 7 (hot)
450°F	230°C	Gas Mark 8 (very hot)
475°F	240°C	Gas Mark 9 (very hot)
500°F	260°C	Gas Mark 10 (extremely hot)
Broil	Broil	Grill

*Electric and gas ovens may be calibrated using celsius. However, for an electric oven, increase celsius setting 10 to 20 degrees when cooking above 160°C. For convection or forced air ovens (gas or electric), lower the temperature setting 25°F/10°C when cooking at all heat levels.

Baking Pan Sizes

Imperial / U.S.	Metric
9x1½-inch round cake pan	22- or 23x4-cm (1.5 L)
9x1½-inch pie plate	22- or 23x4-cm (1 L)
8x8x2-inch square cake pan	20x5-cm (2 L)
9x9x2-inch square cake pan	22- or 23x4.5-cm (2.5 L)
11x7x1½-inch baking pan	28x17x4-cm (2 L)
2-quart rectangular baking pan	30x19x4.5-cm (3 L)
13x9x2-inch baking pan	34x22x4.5-cm (3.5 L)
15x10x1-inch jelly roll pan	40x25x2-cm
9x5x3-inch loaf pan	23x13x8-cm (2 L)
2-quart casserole	2 L

U.S. / Standard Metric Equivalents

⅛ teaspoon = 0.5 ml	⅓ cup = 3 fluid ounces = 75 ml
¼ teaspoon = 1 ml	½ cup = 4 fluid ounces = 125 ml
½ teaspoon = 2 ml	⅔ cup = 5 fluid ounces = 150 ml
1 teaspoon = 5 ml	¾ cup = 6 fluid ounces = 175 ml
1 tablespoon = 15 ml	1 cup = 8 fluid ounces = 250 ml
2 tablespoons = 25 ml	2 cups = 1 pint = 500 ml
¼ cup = 2 fluid ounces = 50 ml	1 quart = 1 litre